Complete Banjo Repair

by Larry Sandberg

Oak Publications
New York/London/Sydney

Music Sales America

DISTRIBUTED BY

HAL•LEONARD®
CORPORATION

7777 W. BLUEMOUND RD. P.O.BOX 13819 MILWAUKEE, WI 53213

Cover photograph © Saga Musical Instruments
325 Corey Way, Suite 111, South San Francisco, CA 94080.
All Rights Reserved. Used by Permission.

Photos on pages 6, 10, 14, 38, 54, 58, 66, 78, 84, and 104 by Herb Wise
Photo on page 18 by Constantinos Andreadis
Unless otherwise credited, all technical photos by Larry Shirkey

Cover design by Iris Weinstein
Book design by Barbara Hoffman
Edited by Peter Pickow

Order No. OK 63628
International Standard Book Number: 0.8256.0227.0
Library of Congress Catalog Card Number: 78-74574

Exclusive Distributors:
Music Sales Corporation
257 Park Avenue South, New York, NY 10010
Music Sales Limited
8/9 Frith Street, London W1V 5TZ England
Music Sales Pty. Limited
120 Rothschild Street, Rosebery, Sydney, NSW 2018, Australia

Printed in the United States of America by
Vicks Lithograph and Printing Corporation

CONTENTS

This book is for everyone who wants to learn about banjos: what they do, how they do it, what to do when something goes wrong, and how to keep things going right. The book is written on several levels. You can tell as you read through that some sections are addressed to the casual player, and others to the professional repair person.

A Fairbanks Whyte Laydie Number Nine.

If you're a beginner looking for your first banjo, you'll find information about how to make a wise choice for your first instrument, stylistically and economically as well.

If you're a new player, you'll find all the lore of setup and tinkering that it takes years of hanging out to learn.

And if you're a professional repair person, I hope you'll find some new insights and techniques. Presumably a banjo expert already knows what's in this book. But the more technical chapters should certainly serve the needs of those repair professionals whose expertise is in violins, band instruments, etc., and who have to learn more about banjos as the instrument continues to renew its popularity.

Caution: As you read through this book, remember that it's been written for a multi-level audience, and that it's up to you to find your own level. For example, there's a slow and detailed chapter on how to change strings. It seems that changing strings should be a simple enough operation. It is, but only after the first time.

On the other hand, complex operations like squaring a fingerboard, or replacing a truss rod, should not be undertaken lightly. They require skill and judgment, and the proper tools as well. If you know yourself well enough to know that you're not about to undertake such a task yourself, then take the technical sections of this book in this spirit: they will teach you about the professional repair person's problems and methods, they will enable you to understand and identify any problems that arise with your own banjo, and they will let you discuss them intelligently with the repair person.

But don't take everything I say as absolute gospel. Different repair persons all have their favorite ways of doing things, and they're not all the same. Many times, but by no means all the time, I've suggested alternative methods. To have done so all the time would have been tedious and confusing. I know of one shop, for example, where each of three repairmen working on adjacent benches favors a different glue, and a different clamping set-up, for replacing a fingerboard. Or one repair person might drill out a peghole where another would use a reamer. Or one might drive in a fifth-string spike where another would drill and glue. And so on, arguing endlessly into the night. Some admit that there is more than one way to do a job, while others hold all those whose methods differ from their own in secret contempt. Or not-so-secret.

While I accept full responsibility for this book, I want to acknowledge the unbegrudging help of those many friends whose advice I accepted and sometimes rejected. Charles Sawtelle of the Hot Rize Bluegrass Band was a pillar of support at the beginning when I needed it most. Nick Forster, Mark Grube, and Rick Kirby of the Denver Folklore Center put up with more pestering than any repairman ought to stand for. David Ferretta (Ferretta Music Service) and Harry Fleischman (D.T.D. Music) made their shops and their personal expertise open to me.

I also want to thank Diana Gilmore, Dave Harrower, Harry Tuft, Dick Weissman, and Dave Wilson for allowing me to use photographs of their instruments. These photos and many of the others in this book were taken by Larry Shirkey. Other illustrations have come through the grace and kindness of the Ome Banjo Company (Ken Whelpton), the Stewart-Macdonald Company,

Saga Musical Instruments, the D'Addario string company, and the C. F. Martin Organisation (Mike Longworth).

Oak Publications granted permission to use a number of illustrations and a short section of Hideo Kamimoto's *Complete Guitar Repair*. I recommend this excellent book to supplement my own in all those aspects of repair and maintenance common to both guitars and banjos. Jason Shulman at Oak encouraged me and saw me through the entire project. At the end, Nancy Clegg, Anne-Marie Rossi, Barbara Davidson, and Carolyn North helped get the manuscript together.

Chapter I
THE PARTS OF THE BANJO

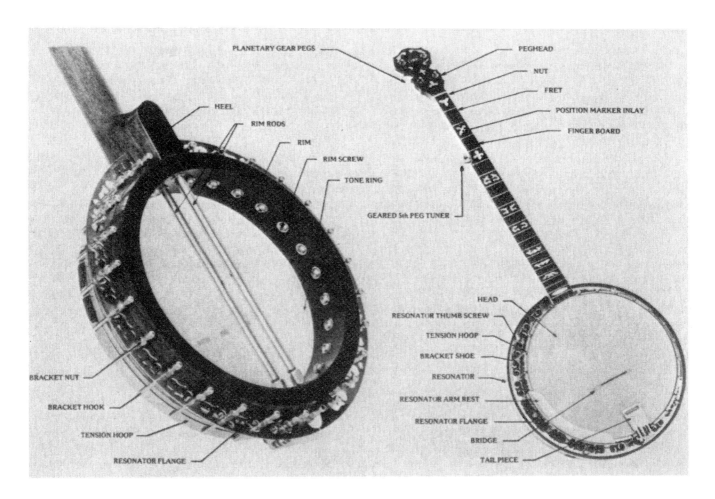

A typical five-string resonator-style banjo, with multi-piece flange and bracket shoes. (Ome Co.)

The photo above shows a pretty typical banjo, but not all banjos are exactly the same. I'll discuss some of the basic design differences in this chapter, but you'll have to check out chapters later on for more illustrations and fuller discussion of the individual parts.

As you look at the banjo, your eye will easily divide it into two sections: the long, thin neck, and the assembly of numerous parts making up the round lower body called the pot. People use the word *neck* loosely to refer to the neck proper along with the *fingerboard* and *peghead* that are joined to it.

Peghead (Headstock)

Starting at the end of the neck we find the peghead, shaped out of the same piece of wood as the neck. In this respect banjo construction is the same as the construction of most steel-string folk guitars. (In classical and flamenco guitars, the peghead is usually shaped out of a separate piece of wood and glue-joined to the neck.) Traditionally, banjo pegheads are carved in ornate shapes and inlaid with the maker's name and other ornamentation. Usually, the top of the peghead is overlaid with a wood veneer, not only for decoration but also to add strength. The peghead provides a place to mount the tuning pegs for the first four strings. Some people use the word **headstock** to mean the same thing as peghead, but sometimes *headstock* just refers to the inlaid veneer overlay of the peghead.

Pegs (Tuners, Tuning Pegs, Gears, Machines)

All these words refer to the **tuning pegs**. The pegs for the first four strings are mounted on the pegboard, while the fifth-string peg is set into the neck near the fifth fret. The banjo pictured above has **planetary geared tuners**, where the gears are enclosed within a widened part of the tuner. Other banjos may have ungeared **friction tuners**, and some very old instruments may still use their original wood or ivory **violin pegs**. Some inexpensive banjos may have exposed **worm and gear tuners** like those on a guitar or mandolin.

Nut

The **nut** is a rectangular block of ivory, bone, wood, or ivoroid plastic, notched with grooves to position the strings.

Frets

The **frets** are the metal strips mounted on the fingerboard at specific intervals. Frets are usually made of nickel alloy; brass frets are softer and wear down faster. Banjo frets are usually narrower than guitar frets, although there was a period during the 1950s when some manufacturers were using guitar-style frets. The standard number of frets on today's banjos is twenty-two.

When you play the banjo, you put your finger down on the string near the fret, not on it. For this reason, the word *fret*, when used to describe playing, actually refers to the space between the metal frets.

Inlays (Position Markers)

Fingerboard **inlays** come in patterns ranging from simple dots to unique carvings that are the product of painstaking craftsmanship. They are usually made of mother-of-pearl, abalone, or pearloid plastic. They aren't merely decorative; they also serve to show you at which fret (or *position*) you're playing. The standard locations are on frets 3,5,7,10,12, and 15. There may be additional inlays on the first and above the fifteenth frets. The tenth-fret position marker is sometimes confusing to players who are used to the guitar since guitars are inlaid at the ninth fret instead.

Fingerboard (Fretboard) and Binding

The **fingerboard** is a wood strip about ¼-inch thick laminated to the wood of the neck. It serves as a mounting surface for the frets. Frets are not mounted directly into the neck wood for several reasons: the best kinds of wood for neck stability are different from the best kinds of woods for mounting frets, and fingerboards get a lot of wear over the years. When they are separate, the fingerboard can be replaced. In addition, the extra layer adds strength to the neck. Some banjos are made with more layers of wood under the fingerboard for even more strength. Rosewood and ebony are used for the fingerboards of the best banjos. Ebony is the harder of the two and resists wear better, but it is a more brittle wood and chips easily when frets are set or replaced. On some banjos the edges of the fingerboard are enclosed in ornamental strips of celluloid **binding** material.

Neck, Heel, and Reinforcing Rod (Truss Rod, Tension Rod)

Maple and mahogany are the woods most commonly used for the necks of fine banjos, but you'll also see plenty of good necks made of walnut, rosewood, and other stable hardwoods that resist warping under pressure from the strings. Most banjos have (and should have) a non-adjustable **reinforcing rod** or an adjustable truss rod (also called a **tension rod**) built into the neck under the fingerboard.

The thick butt end of the neck where it joins up to the pot is called the **heel**. The underside of the heel is sometimes covered with a decorative veneer of fine wood, ivory, etc. called a **heel plate**. Most people, including myself, call the end of the neck and fingerboard closest to the peghead the *lower end*, and the end of the neck and fingerboard closest to the pot the *higher end*. This reflects the playing point of view, since it refers to the pitch getting higher or lower relative to the position that you fret the strings. This terminology isn't standardized, however, and some people mean just the opposite when they say higher or lower.

Head (Skin)

The **head** is a replaceable membrane of calfskin or mylar plastic that picks up and amplifies the vibrations of the plucked strings. It is stretched taut over the top of the pot.

Tension Hoop, Bracket Hooks, and Bracket Nuts

The **tension hoop** (also called a **stretcher band**) fits over the edge or collar of the head and stretches the head taut as the **bracket hooks** are tightened by screwing down the **bracket nuts**.

Rim (Shell)

The **rim** is the circular structure that forms the main part of the pot assembly. All the other parts are in some way attached to it. Most good rims are built up of laminations of maple and/or beech, but there are other kinds of rim design (such as cast aluminum) which also give a good sound.

Bracket Shoes and Rim Screws

The **bracket shoes** provide a bearing surface for the bracket nuts as they tighten the bracket hooks. They are attached to the rim by the **rim screws** (also called **shoe screws**). On the particular banjo pictured at the beginning of this chapter, there is also a **flange**, which is held in place between the bracket nuts and the bracket shoes. On other banjos there are no bracket shoes at all. Instead, the bracket nuts tighten against the flange, which in turn rests against a protruding wooden lip machined out of the rim.

Flange (Resonator Flange, Flange-Plate)

The **flange** is mainly a decorative space-filler between the rim and the sides of the resonator. On the banjo pictured, the flange plate attaches to the bracket assembly. On other banjos, the flange mounts against a protruding lip machined into the rim and there are no bracket shoes. Such banjos may have either a **one-piece flange** consisting of a very heavy flange-plate, or a **two-piece**

flange consisting of a thin flange-plate supported by a strong hollow tube which rests against the lip and bears the pressure of the bracket assembly. On banjos with no resonator, there is no flange.

Armrest

The **armrest** makes playing more comfortable, and also protects the head from wear by the forearm. If your banjo doesn't have one, you can easily buy one from a music store or parts supplier.

Bridge

The hardwood **bridge** transmits sound vibrations from the plucked string to the head, and is grooved to position the strings. Standard bridge heights are 1/2-inch and 5/8-inch. Which size to use depends on the way your particular banjo has been built and set up.

Tailpiece

The primary function of the **tailpiece** is to hold the strings. In addition, some tailpieces are adjustable to control the tension and the angle of the string against the bridge. This affects tone and volume. Almost all tailpieces are attached by a bracket to a bracket-shoe or to the flange, but a few are mounted on the rim.

Tone Ring (Head Bearing)

The **tone ring** is not really visible in the photo, but the arrow points to its general location. It is a metal collar that sits on top of the rim, so that the head can be tightened against it. Tone rings come in a variety of designs which significantly affect the tone and volume of the banjo. On cast aluminum rims, the tone ring and rim are cast as one piece.

Resonator

The **resonator** is the sound-reflecting plate that fits over the back of the rim. Resonators not only add volume but also affect tonal and sustaining characteristics. You need a resonator to get the true bluegrass sound, but old-time pickers and frailers prefer the sound of an open-back banjo with no resonator.

Chapter II

BANJO SOUND

A string vibrates in several complex patterns at the same time. Pluck a string and you'll notice a combination of two components: movement parallel to the banjo head, and movement perpendicular to the head. The ratio between the two components can vary depending on the angle with which your finger strikes the string. This makes for a difference in tone. Different people hold their hands differently when they play. This difference in the angle of finger attack is the main reason why two different players can sound so different even when they trade off on the same banjo.

Harmonics

In addition, there are a whole set of other complex movements going on within the vibrating arc of the string. They are hard to see as you

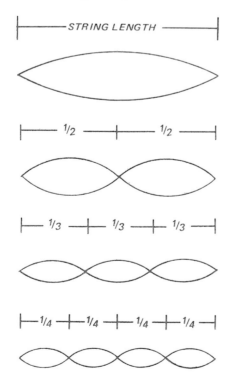

Sections of a vibrating string.

watch the string, but they show up on measuring devices like an oscilloscope. What happens is that the string vibrates not only as a whole, but also in fractional parts; along its whole length and also by halves, thirds, quarters, and so on.

The diagram above shows only the first few of these possible subdivisions of vibration. The human ear—and only the most sensitive ear at that—can perceive the sound waves of the smaller arcs only down to about 1/16 of the length of the vibrating string. The sounds of the smaller arcs are called *harmonics*, *partials*, or *overtones*. They are produced by all instruments. In wind instruments the harmonics are produced by vibrating subdivisions of the air column. Any given instrument, by nature of its structure and materials, tends to reinforce some harmonics and supress others. This is what makes the same note of a given pitch sound different on a guitar, banjo, oboe or what have you.

The vibration of the total length of the string is called the *fundamental* or *fundamental tone*. Take the G string, for example: Pluck it and you'll hear mainly the sound of the fundamental, G. But since the string is also vibrating in partials, you'll hear in addition to the fundamental:

1) Another G, an octave above the fundamental, produced by the vibrating half-length.
2) A high D note, produced by the vibrating thirds of the total arc.
3) Another G, two octaves above the fundamental, produced by the vibrating quarters of the string arc.
4) A high B note, produced by the vibrating fifths of the total string arc.

And so on, in smaller and smaller fractions, so that the sound of any given note produced by any musical instrument is actually a rich combination of the fundamental and the numerous overtones. Of these numerous overtones produced by the vibrating string, air column, etc., some will be reinforced and some suppressed by the nature of the structure and materials of the individual instrument, so that each instrument has its own unique *tone color* or *timbre*. A pure fundamental tone can only be produced by electronic means. Even the flute, which has the strongest fundamental of all instruments, still has some overtones.

Think of a calm ocean, with regularly undulating waves bobbing evenly up and down. This corresponds roughly to a fundamental without overtones. Acoustic scientists call it a *pure tone.* It's a relatively characterless sound, and makes for uninteresting music.

Now think of a choppy sea, with large billows composed of smaller wavelets that ride across them. This is what the sound of a musical instrument is like. This combination of harmonic partials along with the fundamental is what acoustic scientists call a *compound tone.*

One kind of instrument sounds different from another because of the different partials that it reinforces or suppresses. But it's also the case that different models of the same instrument can sound different, since the choice of different materials and design will have an effect on the particular combination of overtones that a given instrument produces. And this is why it will be so important to talk about all the aspects of size, construction, design, and materials with which this book is concerned.

Old Strings

The strings themselves are terribly important too, since they do the actual work of vibrating. When your strings get old from metal fatigue, distortion, and corrosion, or if they are imperfectly made, the upper partials become impure and irregular. In a manner of speaking, the string goes out of tune with itself. This is why old strings sound bad and are difficult to tune.

What Makes a Banjo Sound Good?

When you play, the vibrations of the string pass down through the bridge onto the surface of the head. These vibrations set the head in motion, and it amplifies the sound. In the language of acoustics, the head is a *sounding board.* The sound is amplified even more by the vibrations of air within the *semi-enclosed air chamber* formed inside the pot. The presence or absence of a resonator alters the acoustic properties of this air chamber.

But the story doesn't end there. Sound waves are absorbed and/or reflected back to the head by the entire structure of the banjo—mainly by the pot, but even by the neck as well. Some materials sound better than others, though to a certain extent just what "better" means is determined by your own taste as well as by general social standards. Changing over from a maple to a mahogany neck will probably lead to a discernible tone difference, which a given player might or might not prefer. On the other hand, almost everyone will agree that banjos with brass tone rings, tension hoops, etc. sound better than banjos with cast-steel or white-metal parts. It's also the case that heavier banjos tend to be the ones that sound best. Brass and good hardwoods weigh a lot, and vibrating air chambers work best when surrounded by a very rigid enclosure. However, a heavy banjo that is poorly designed and assembled won't necessarily sound as good as a well-made lightweight instrument. What you need to take with you when you go banjo shopping is a good pair of ears, not a pair of scales.

What Makes Good Banjos So Expensive?

Good quality woods are expensive. Good quality metals are expensive. And since time is expensive, so is workmanship. Wood joining and metal casting must be done with care. Dies and molds must be designed. And above all else, the banjo must be assembled with care. The most important factor in good banjo sound is that all parts must be well fitted, so that sound waves can pass evenly and unimpeded throughout the instrument. The neck should abut the rim tightly and stably. The head should be level and equally tight across its entire surface. This is partly a function of how well you mount it, but you just can't mount it well if the rim, tone ring, and tension hoop are out of round or of a poor fit. All parts need to be snug and free of dirt and corrosion.

So what you pay for are good-quality materials and good-quality workmanship and attention. In addition, the consumer market for good-quality banjos also demands fancy banjos, well-finished and with attractive inlay work. If you add fine woodcarving of the neck heel, say, or engraving of the metal parts, you're left with a pretty substantial bill for labor.

Varieties of Banjo Sound

Throughout this book we'll be talking about banjo sound in terms of two opposite extremes. One is the thick, plunky, woody sound favored by old-time players, mostly for the clawhammer and frailing styles. People who go for this sound generally don't wear fingerpicks and play close to the neck. The other sound is bright, piercing, metallic, and a little thinner. People who go for this sound generally do wear fingerpicks and play close to the bridge. This is the contemporary bluegrass sound. There are also numerous compromises along the spectrum between these two sounds. The classic bluegrass sound of Earl Scruggs, for example, is relatively dark and plunky, but still not that much so that most old-time players would be happy with Earl's banjo.

Remember, though, that although parts changes and adjustments can change the sound of your banjo, they can do so only within limits. There are people who love to tinker with their banjos just as other people are always tinkering with their cars. But if you're basically unhappy with your banjo, your best bet is to start looking for a new one. And no amount of tinkering can replace practising.

Chapter III
INTONATION, SCALE, AND BRIDGE PLACEMENT

Playing in Tune

The ability of a player, singer, or an instrument itself to stay in tune is called *intonation*. Your job as a banjo player is to get your strings as perfectly in tune as you can, and to replace them when they get old and dirty enough that you can't do so any longer. You must also make sure that your bridge is in the right place at all times. By the way, don't let yourself get upset by a funny kind of tuning paranoia that may come over you somewhere along the early road between being a beginner and starting to turn into a real player. You may notice that in spite of experience your banjo is becoming harder instead of easier to get in tune. What is probably happening is that your ear is beginning to notice all kinds of sloppy tuning that you were oblivious to before. I've often seen this happen.

If your job is to get your instrument in tune, the maker's job is to build you an instrument that you can get in tune in the first place. This means simply that the frets have to be placed at precisely the correct intervals. Take a good look at the frets on your instrument. You'll notice that they aren't equidistant from each other. Rather, they get closer and closer together as you look further up the fingerboard. We'll have to dip into the science of acoustics to see why this should be so. I've tried to make the following discussion as simple as possible, even to the point of indulging in some oversimplification. Still, it's impossible to get by without some mathematics, since mathematics is the physical basis of music.

For a full discussion of the problems of tuning, I recommend the Oak book, *How to Tune Your Guitar*. For a more serious excursion, try the articles, "Temperament" and "Intervals, calculations of" in the *Harvard Dictionary of Music*. And if you're professionally trained in math and physics, you might enjoy a trip through Helmholtz's *The Perception of Tone*.

The Octave

Our whole system of music is based on a series of twelve notes. (Technically speaking the word *note* should be used of the dot on the printed page, and the word *pitch* or *tone* should be used to talk about what you hear. But most folks use the word *note* loosely to refer also to what you hear, and I will too.)

Out of these twelve notes that are the basis for our system, seven of them go to make up the scale that we've all heard a million times: do, re, mi, fa, sol, la, ti, do. I've just listed a total of eight notes, but only seven are different. The last is the same as the first. You repeat yourself and start all over again at that point. The range of sound encompassed by these eight notes is called an *octave* (from the Latin *octo*, meaning "eight").

Try playing a scale on your banjo. You can do it starting on any string, but let's do it on the third, since this will sound most natural in terms of the way the whole instrument is tuned. Since we're starting on the G string, we'll be playing a G scale. You can play the scale with any one finger of your left hand, though you're welcome to work out fancier fingerings if you feel like it. Just play the following frets: open, second, fourth, fifth, seventh, ninth, eleventh, and twelfth. Try to sing along with it; it's the good old do-re-mi scale, with the eight notes spread out across twelve frets to encompass an octave's worth of sound.

Now the interesting thing about an octave is that it's not merely some fabrication of a mathematically fevered brain. It's solidly rooted in physical reality. That distance of twelve frets that you've just covered happens to be half of the total length of the vibrating string. Try measuring the distance of the whole string from the nut to the bridge. This distance is called the *scale*. Most banjos have a scale length of 26 to 26½ inches depending on the model, and some unusual banjos may be a bit longer or shorter. Whatever the total scale length of your banjo happens to be, the 12th fret should be in the middle. If it isn't, that means that your bridge is in the wrong place, and should be moved. More about this a little later on.

If an octave takes up one-half the length of the vibrating string, then the *next* octave is going to have to take up one-half the space of the *remaining* length of the string above the 12th fret. So the amount of space encompassed by an octave grows smaller by one-half with each successive octave that you move up the string. The frets have to be laid out to express this diminishing proportion. That's why the distance between them grows smaller and smaller as you move on up the fingerboard.

When you sit down and try to work out the math that will tell you exactly where to place the frets, though, you run into a serious problem. It's one that instrument makers have never been able to solve completely. It turns out that if you compute the exact proportions based on this reasoning, you'll wind up with your octaves sure enough in tune, but with some of the notes within the octave seriously out of tune with some of the others. This problem exists on all instruments that are called *fixed pitch* instruments: guitars and banjos, where you have frets; pianos, where you have a fixed string-length; oboes and clarinets, where you have to bore holes at fixed distances; and so on. It's not a problem for fiddlers, though, since they can slide their fingers around, and it's not a problem for singers since they can slide their voices around.

Over the past hundreds of years, theoreticians and instrument makers have tried several ways of monkeying around with changes in the mathematical proportions of fret placement in order to at least minimize this problem, even though it cannot be solved completely. These different ways of tuning are called *temperaments.* The system that has been favored from the late 1700s up to the present day is called *equal temperament.* It represents a compromise. In the other systems, some notes were made perfectly in tune at the expense of others which were badly out of tune. In equal temperament, all the notes are slightly out of tune. We've become so used to it that it doesn't bother us. In fact, we've become so used to equal temperament that very often when we hear folk or primitive music being sung or played in a different temperament, we perceive it as being out of tune, rather than as being perfectly executed according to a different standard of intonation.

The usual procedure for positioning the frets on guitars, banjos, etc. is to divide the scale length—the length of the vibrating string—by 17.817. After the first fret is mounted 1/17.817 of the way up the fingerboard, you then divide the *remaining* length of the string by 17.817 to position the second fret, and so on. I have not yet seen a banjo on which the maker did so careless a job of positioning the frets that the instrument failed to play in tune, but the possibility certainly does exist. The only cure would be to replace the fingerboard and refret it accurately.

It's a fair assumption that the maker did his job. If your banjo plays out of tune when you play chords and single notes up and down the neck, and if your strings are not very old and your action is good, then your bridge is most likely set in the wrong place. It's easy enough for this to happen. If your bridge is even a fraction of an inch away from where it should be, you've got a serious problem on your hands since the maker's proportion for laying out the frets no longer holds true.

Placing the Bridge

Finding the correct spot for the bridge is the easiest thing in the world; even if you have no understanding of the underlying *why, what* to do is very simple. All you need to do is to measure the distance from the end of the nut (the point at which the vibrating string leaves the edge of the nut) up to the middle of the 12th fret. This will be somewhere between 12¾ and 13½ inches unless you have a rather unusual banjo. Whatever that length is, your bridge should be the same distance from the 12th fret. Simply measure that distance, and set your bridge roughly in the correct spot.

Roughly in the correct spot. Don't kill yourself to be within more than, say, 1/32-inch tolerance, if that. This is because you have to take into account the slight stretching of the string-length that occurs when you press the string down to fret it. Most bridges actually need to be set the tiniest bit back from the "correct" position (as determined by a straightedge measure) in order to compensate for this stretching. Just how small an alteration to make depends on the action of your particular banjo, and the only way to tell exactly is by playing and listening. If you note consistently sharp, you need to lengthen the vibrating part of the string by pushing the bridge back a little, toward the tailpiece. Too flat, and you need to move the bridge forward, toward the neck.

Bridge Compensation.

The story doesn't end here even if your frets are perfectly mounted and your bridge is perfectly placed. You may still be having intonation problems as you play up and down the fingerboard, this time caused by some built-in discrepancies in the nature of string manufacture. Steel strings are so very sensitive to the slightest disproportion that even so small a factor as the difference in their diameters as you go from string to string may cause the instrument to play out of tune. The problem is usually most noticeable on the third string. In order to cure it, you must *compensate* your bridge.

A rough but simple way to compensate your bridge is to set it on a slight angle under the strings, with the side under the first string pushed a bit forward towards the fingerboard and the side under the fifth string pushed a bit backwards towards the tailpiece. Theoretically this is an abomination. Wound and unwound strings behave differently, and ideally the wound fourth string should be forward of the third. But, *in practise*, a lot of players have found that this slanting of the bridge solves their problems. It depends partly on your style: If you do most of your up-the-neck playing without using the fourth string too much, and if you're not one of the relatively few players who fret the fifth string, then you can probably get away with slanting the bridge.

Only recently has an alternative solution appeared in the form of a *compensated saddle* that the Shubb Capo Company has been marketing. It is to be expected that other companies will soon market their own designs as well. The compensated saddle may not be necessary for all players or all banjos, but it certainly represents the most effective solution to the problems of intonation caused by string-gauge discrepancies. Take care if you use one, since a compensated banjo bridge is fragile by nature.

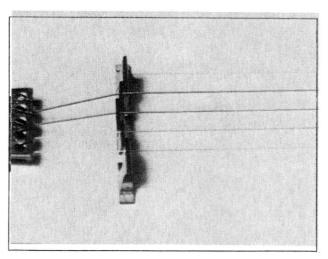

A compensated bridge.

Chapter IV
TUNING PEGS

Good tuners are worth having; they will certainly improve the quality of your musical life. Most banjos need upgrading in the way of tuners; good ones are expensive, and one way for a manufacturer to cut costs on an otherwise pretty fair quality banjo is to mount second-rate tuners. On a real cheapie banjo, though, the cost of good tuners may be disproportionate to your original investment. In that case, don't bother. You also have to consider the weight of good tuners. They can get to be pretty heavy. If you have a banjo with a lightweight rim and you mostly play it in your lap rather than with a strap, heavy tuners may pull it out of balance and make it hard to hold. However, the weight of the tuners can also have an acoustic side effect: The banjo's ability to sustain a note is often increased slightly with heavier tuners.

Good-quality tuners should give you a sense of stability when you tune. The gears will be tight and true, so that the pitch of the string won't change when you remove your hand from the tuning knob. They should also have a fairly high gear ratio. This means that one complete revolution of the knob will produce only a fraction of a revolution of the shaft (also called the barrel) around which the string is wound. This gives you a much more sensitive pitch-adjustment and makes it much easier to keep your banjo in tune. A 4:1 ratio feels real good, but the 2:1 ratio of lighter and less expensive tuners works well too. There are four basic types of tuning mechanism: Friction pegs, geared tuners, worm-and-gear tuners, and violin tuners.

Friction Pegs

The friction peg is cheap and simple. It consists of a *shaft*, a metal *collar*, and a *knob* to turn the shaft. The knob is held onto the shaft with a screw which, when turned, tightens the assembly in its hole in the peghead. This friction keeps the tuner from loosening in response to the pressure of the string. You need to adjust the screw just enough to hold the string steady, but not so much that the peg is too hard to turn. These screws are always working themselves loose, so you need to have a screwdriver in your case at all times if you own this kind of tuner.

Since there is no gear, the knob turns the shaft on a 1:1 ratio, and you can never get the degree of finesse in tuning that geared tuners offer. Nonetheless, many folks are pretty happy with their friction tuners. Often it makes sense to keep friction tuners on a fine old banjo merely for the sake of preserving its original condition. Some of the old tuners had characteristic knobs of wood, ivory, or plastic in shapes that you just can't get anymore. In order to preserve the original appearance of the banjo as much as possible if you do go to geared tuners, get a set of new tuners with a compatible shaft so you can transfer the knobs.

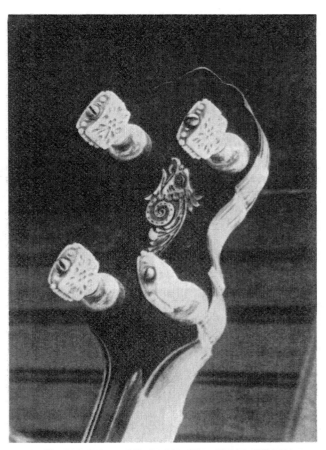

Geared tuners on a Fairbanks Whyte Laydie. The original engraved ivory friction pegs have been remounted on geared tuners.

On old instruments, the friction tuner may have enlarged its hole with the passage of time. In this case, you need to fill in the old hole with a hardwood plug and then drill out a new hole. This procedure is described fully in the section on violin tuners below.

Geared Tuners

You can recognize these tuners by the enclosed gear housing built into the collar.

Geared tuners. The lower middle tuner is for the fifth string. Note the mounting screws and positioning stud on several of the tuners.

The housing encloses a set of planetary gear cogs sealed in lubricant.

The inner life of a planetary geared tuner.

Since the housing is completely enclosed, no lubrication maintenance is needed. This design was originally produced by the Planet Company, but other companies make the planetary design as well. *Planet* is a brand name; *planetary* is the general technical name for this kind of gearbox.

Some planetary gears mount simply in the peghead hole. Others are further stabilized by a mounting screw or a positioning stud, which need to have a hole drilled out with a fine bit on a drill or Dremel tool.

The collar which passes through the peghead hole is usually of greater diameter on geared tuners than it is on friction tuners, so if you convert from friction pegs you will probably need to enlarge the hole. A straight reamer is the best tool for the job. Drilling is also possible, but even if you drill from the top of the peghead, as you should, you always run more risk of chipping out some wood, especially from the peghead overlay, than you do by reaming. As with all peg mounting work, take care to keep the hole absolutely perpendicular to the plane of the peghead.

The knob, like that of friction tuners, is attached to the shaft by a screw that controls the resistance of the tuner to string pressure. It needs to be not too tight and not too loose; you can easily feel out the correct setting by experimenting. Usually there will be a washer-like spring under the screw head to help provide tension for a good set.

The bass-side and treble-side tuners have opposite gears and can't be switched around.

Worm-and-Gear Tuners

These are the kind of tuners that you see on guitars and mandolins. They are not traditional for banjos, but some companies (notably the Harmony Company) have used them anyway. It's a good idea to lubricate this kind of tuner with a small application of grease or oil once or twice a year. Occasionally a gear strips from wear: perhaps the gear-holding screw has not been kept tight enough, or the knob-shaft has been bent, and so the cog and worm have not been meshing evenly. Since cost is minimal, the easiest thing to do is to replace the whole assembly. As with planet tuners, the machines for the bass and treble sides have opposite gears and cannot be interchanged.

As a rule, banjos with worm-and-gear tuners are cheapies and not really worth the trouble of cosmetic alternation to friction or planetary pegs. If you do make such an alteration, you'll be left with the old holes from the screws that mounted the worm-and-gear tuners to the side of the peg-head. Such holes can be filled according to traditional practise with plugs cut from hardwood dowel, then spot-finished. Recently, repair persons have been experimenting with new methods for repairing such small defects that involve filling the hole with dyed epoxy or cyanoacrylate glue instead.

Violin Tuners.

These tapered wood shafts, held in place solely by friction in the peghead hole, are still to be found on very old banjos. They are also used on many of the modern fretless banjos made by cottage industries in the Southeast.

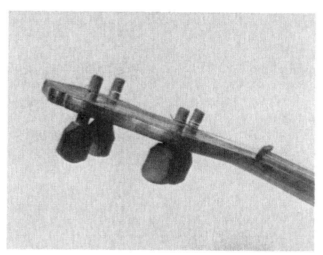
Violin-style pegs on a modern fretless banjo.

Sometimes ivory was used, and on fine early banjos, the pegs were ornately carved and engraved. Such pegs should be preserved.

Violin tuners are a royal pain to keep in tune with steel strings, but somewhat easier with the nylon strings that most folks like on their fretless banjos. Nonetheless, they are so visually pleasing that they may be worth keeping for that reason alone. And if the banjo in question is not going to be used in professional situations where long tuning episodes are a hassle, the problem loses importance. However, the pegs must be well fitted in order to minimize frustration. It also helps to rub down the shaft with a product called *peg dope* which is available from violin shops. It does the same thing that the right wax does for a pair of skis: provides smoothness when you need it (as you turn the peg) and friction when you need it (when you let go of the peg and it has to resist string pressure).

Learning how to turn friction pegs is an art in itself. You need to push the peg slightly upward in its tapered hole as you turn it, so that it maintains friction against the peghead wood and doesn't lose its grip. But you can't push too hard, or else it will catch by friction and make fine tuning impossible. The easiest way is to turn the peg with your left hand while pressing down on the top of the peghead with your right. One-handed tuning of violin-style pegs is a proud accomplishment.

Well-fitted pegs require a hole tapered absolutely true to the taper of the peg-shaft itself. In an old instrument, wear may have altered the original taper of the hole. If the hole is not too far gone, the situation can be corrected by adjusting the hole with a tapered reamer. Reamers of the correct range of sizes are available from violin shops and suppliers.

In addition, new or old peg tapers can be adjusted by turning the peg in a violin peg shaper. This tool is essentially a large version of the razor-blade type of pencil sharpener that you used to carry in your pencil box when you were in school. They don't work, though, for ivory pegs, which must be sanded by hand or put on a lathe.

Turning a violin peg in a peg-shaper. (H. Kamimoto)

If a peg is lost or must be replaced, a new one can easily be obtained from a violin shop. Sometimes it isn't possible to find an exact match for old pegs, in which case you may want to replace all four or five of them for visual consistency. Pegs are available in black ebony, dark brown rosewood, or light brown boxwood. You can also find flamenco guitar pegs, which usually carry an extra bit of ornamentation on the knob. Most flamenco guitar pegs come with a smaller diameter shaft than violin pegs, however.

21

Sometimes the peghole becomes so worn that you have to plug it and start all over again with a new hole. For visual consistency many repair persons prefer to cut a plug out of the same kind of wood as the original peghead wood, with similar grain and coloration. The trick is to use a tapered plug that will fit in under the peghead overlay. That way you can ream out the peghead wood under the overlay without disturbing the overlay itself very much, so that the plug will not be easily visible from the top of the peghead.

If sightliness is not an issue, or if you're prepared to refinish or replace the overlay, then there's an easier alternative. Simply drill or ream out the old hole (with a straight reamer) to accommodate a section of hardwood dowelling. Once the plug or dowel is glued in, you simply drill and ream it out true to the taper of the peg.

Fifth-String Pegs

I strongly recommend that you equip your banjo with one or another brand of geared fifth-string tuner even if you keep friction pegs on your first four strings. You'll save yourself an awful lot of tuning hassle that way.

Fifth-string tuners are mounted in the side of the neck near the 5th fret, just below the point where the fifth-string lip is shaped out of the neck. The string itself bears on a grooved ivory or plastic button mounted in the fingerboard at the beginning of the lip. In an emergency, this button can be replaced with a slotted round-head screw, but the tone of the string against a metal bearing surface is usually too unpleasant for this to be considered a permanent measure.

Most fifth-string tuners are mounted in a crenellated tapered base that grips the sides of the mounting hole pretty well (see photo, page 20). Some brands of tuner provide additional stability in the way of a mounting screw or positioning stud, the hole for which must be drilled out with a fine bit in the Dremel tool. With tuners that don't have a screw or stud—particularly friction tuners—it often happens that over a period of years the base jiggles around in its hole and eventually becomes loose. You may be able to find a different tuner with a larger base. Otherwise the solution is to drill or ream out the hole to accommodate a hardwood dowel. Once the dowel is glued in, drill and ream out a new hole and re-mount the tuner. I have seen people resort to filling in the edges of an enlarged hole with celluloid wood-filler as an emergency measure. This uncraftsmanlike expedient is visually unsatisfying and doesn't last too long.

High-Tuning the Fifth String

Whenever you put a capo on the banjo, you must also tune up the fifth string a corresponding number of frets. However, tuning the fifth string much higher than A (two frets higher than usual) is likely to break it. Besides, constant retuning can be a hassle. For these reasons, people who play a lot in high keys need to have either tuning spikes or a sliding fifth-string capo mounted on the fingerboard.

Tuning Spikes

The tuning spike is made from an L-shaped HO-gauge model railroad spike, easily available from hobby shops. The idea is to set the spike into the fingerboard so that you can slip the string under the L-angle. This holds the string down against a higher fret, raising it in pitch.

The short side of the L is longer than it needs to be, so you can nip it down to almost half its original length. Make sure that all edges are sanded smooth: a jagged surface will lead to broken strings.

For easy tuning to the keys of A and B, many people prefer to use spikes at the 7th and 9th frets. However, you wind up stretching the string a bit whenever you slip it under the spike and will have to make fine adjustments with the tuning peg. Since you need to tune anyway, I've found that just one spike at the 9th fret is really all you need.

Mount the spike about 1/4 of the way down from the 9th fret (towards the 8th) and facing inwards, so that you'll be pulling the fifth string down towards the fourth in order to slide it under the L. The spike should not be directly underneath the fifth string, but rather about 1/16-inch down towards the fourth.

Some repair persons feel secure about driving the spike right in, but you minimize the danger of splitting or chipping the fingerboard if you first drill out a small hole with a fine bit in the Dremel tool. Ebony is quite susceptible to chipping on a job like this, especially if it's old. Drill through the fingerboard but not into the neck wood, so that the point of the spike can take in the neck. Coat the spike in glue—polyvinyl or aliphatic resin will to the job. Don't hammer the spike directly, or you'll bend the angle out of shape. Hammer a nail-set, punch, etc. positioned directly over the spike-shaft. You can then work the spike into its final shape and position with a small screwdriver.

Fifth-String Capos

I've always found fifth-string capos to be rather unsightly, and so would hate to mount one on a beautiful old instrument. However, they can't be beat for the kind of rapid retuning of the fifth string that you have to do in professional situations.

The fifth-string capo is essentially a sliding arm that can fret the fifth string at any of several frets.

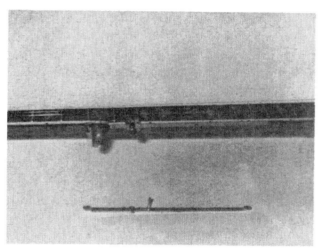

Two kinds of fifth-string capo.

It moves along a shaft which is screw-mounted to the edge or binding of the fingerboard just above the fifth-string peg, where the fingerboard lip begins. Further details and refinements in design vary according to the manufacturer. For mounting, hold the capo to position and scribe the screw-hole locations with a pointed tool; then drill them out with a fine bit in the Dremel tool and mount the capo.

D-Tuners

The original D-tuners were the "Scruggs-peg" design originally developed by Earl Scruggs as a dependable way of getting back and forth be-

tween G and D tunings with a novelty glissando effect.

In the original design, extra pegs were mounted in the headstock between the first- and second-string pegs and between the third- and fourth-string pegs. A cam set in the hole of the shaft held the strings to D tuning.

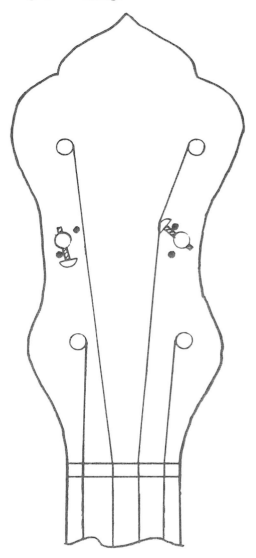

Cam-type Scruggs tuners, showing fourth string in low position and third string in high position. The small solid dots represent studs that circumscribe the arc of the cam.

Various shapes of cam were used; the simplest was just a screw or slot-head bolt with the string set firmly in the slot. Additional nails or studs were driven into the peghead to circumscribe the arc of the cam, so that the pegs when tuned up would move the cam only so far: up to B on the second string and to G on the third string. Turning the pegs back down lowered the strings to A and F♯ respectively.

The above discussion has been couched in the past tense because the original Scruggs design has been superceded for many years by the Bill Keith design. The Keith design incorporates the D-tuning mechanism into the gearshaft of the second- and third-string pegs themselves. (Keith-pegs are available from the Beacon Banjo Company, and other companies have marketed competing designs.) Keith-tuners are expensive. Nonetheless, with their advent, there is no longer any excuse to deface a peghead with tuners of the original Scruggs design.

You need D-tuners to accurately reproduce certain classic Scruggs pieces, as well as for novelty effects such as Keith's "Auld Lang Syne" played entirely with the tuners. But you should seriously question how important these effects are for *you* before you get involved in the trouble and expense of D-tuners. Many first-rate players live very happily without them.

Chapter V
STRINGS

Loop End vs. Ball End

Banjo strings come in two varieties: *loop end* and *ball end.* The kind of string you need depends on the kind of tailpiece you have. Many tailpieces accept both kinds, but some accept only one or the other.

You can easily recognize loop-end strings from the loop, where one end of the string winds around itself forming something like a hangman's noose. Some strings have a decorative fuzzy cloth filament wrapped in with the winding and some don't; there's no big difference. These strings fit over tailpieces that have some kind of hook for the loop to grab.

Ball-end strings also have a loop, but the loop comes wound around a *ball.* The "ball" is actually a small, hollow, barrel-shaped cylinder with grooved edges for the string to fit around.

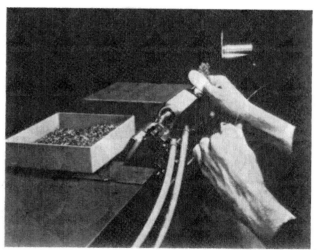

Attaching the barrels to ball-end strings. (D'Addario Co.)

Ball-end tailpieces have some kind of protruding edge that the ball fits under, and a hole or groove for the string to come through. The pressure of the tightened string will hold the ball flush against the tailpiece.

Every so often you may find yourself in an emergency situation where the only kind of replacement available is the wrong kind. With a little ingenuity you can muddle through.

You can convert loop-end to ball-end strings simply by finding some object to make an emergency ball out of. A nail, a piece of baling wire, a safety pin—anything will do as long as it holds the tightened string in place. Try to find something that won't put too much of a sharp bend in the loop as it is tightened up. The sharper the kink, the faster the string will break at that point.

Converting ball-end to loop-end is harder. With luck you may be able to work the ball out of the loop without destroying it. You shouldn't be able to do this on a well-made string, but a good many don't come as tightly wound around the ball as they should. Otherwise, try doubling the string around through the hole in the ball. You'll wind up with a rather awkward new loop that may or may not fit your tailpiece depending on its particular design.

Old Strings

After a while your strings will build up an accumulation of dead finger tissue, grow corroded from sweat, and become distorted from playing pressure. You might find it necessary to change strings anywhere from once a week to once in several months depending on how much you sweat at the fingertips, how much time you spend playing, what kind of tone you want, and what kind of tone your banjo gives you. You can make your strings last a little longer by wiping down the strings, neck, and fingerboard with a clean, soft cloth at the end of each playing session.

Another trick that seems to add a little extra life to dirty strings is to loosen them one at a time and then wipe them down with a rag wet with rubbing alcohol. Make sure you get the underside of the string clean, since this is where dead skin tissue and sweat deposits tend to accumulate. The purpose of loosening the strings is to enable you to get underneath without getting a lot of alcohol on the fingerboard. If the strings aren't too far gone to begin with, they'll sound a little better after you clean them off. Or at least they often do to me, though some friends tell me that I'm suffering from autosuggestion. . .

No matter what you do, the day will come when you have to change strings. The final stage of string aging is one of complete hopelessness and despair, when you can't get your instrument in tune and nothing sounds good and you don't even feel like playing. A long overdue string change can brighten up your whole musical life. Or perhaps your fourth-string winding is coming loose, or you've broken a string. Here's how to change strings:

Changing Strings

It's easiest to change strings one at a time, because that way the other strings will keep the bridge in place. It's also a little better for the neck if you maintain string pressure instead of taking them all off at once. Don't leap to the other extreme, though, and become afraid of removing all the strings. You'll find that your banjo feels better if every so often you take off all the strings at once so you can clean off the fingerboard with some 0000-grade steel wool and a little lemon oil, violin polish, boiled linseed oil, etc. A clean fingerboard is more fun to play on, and in fact the accumulation of dead tissue can build up to the point where it makes sliding the fingers awkward and otherwise impedes technique. I like to do this once a year or so, but I don't sweat much: you might want to do it more often. If you do take all the strings off at once, make sure that you mark the correct bridge position on the head in pencil or with tape, to save yourself the trouble of having to measure for it later on.

The first step in changing a string is to remove the old string. You can simply tune down the peg until the string can be pulled off. I've always found it a little easier to tune the string pretty low and then cut it about 3/4 of the way towards the nut with a nipper or cutting pliers. That makes it much easier to get the string out of most tailpieces. Be careful of your eyes during the whole process of changing strings.

Now its time for the new string. Getting it wound properly is important, since a carelessly wound string will slip around a lot and take hours or days of stretching before it stays in tune. Careless winding can also lead to prematurely broken strings. Experienced players tend to develop their own peculiar style of putting on strings, some with the ease of a ballerina and others with the ferocious intensity of a Russian weight-lifter. It helps to keep the instrument placed in some stable and orderly position: on a padded bench surface supported by a neck rest, or securely on your lap, or with the pot resting on the floor and the neck held between your knees.

Begin by engaging the ball or loop of the string with the tailpiece. Many tailpiece designs are such that you will have to hold the string slightly taut from this point on in order to keep it from slipping off. In any case, the string will wind more securely if you keep it slightly taut no matter what tailpiece design you have.

Holding the string in your right hand, run it across the fingerboard and over the nut and through the hole in the tuning peg shaft. Don't worry about the bridge; the string will pull into its final position when you tighten it up. The string should go into the hole in the shaft from the inside of the headstock, rather than the outer edge. This means that to tighten the string you'll be turning the pegs clockwise for the third and fourth strings; counterclockwise for the first and second strings. The shaft for the fifth-string peg might be either parallel or perpendicular to the fingerboard depending on the kind of brand of peg you have. In any case, insert the string so that you will be tightening it by turning the peg counterclockwise. Make sure that you wind your strings in the right direction. Putting your strings in through the shaft from the wrong side will angle them too sharply off the nut when they are tightened, and lead to premature breakage. In addition, you'll be turning the pegs in the opposite direction than that to which people are accustomed, which can cause no end of confusion.

Holding the end of the string through the shaft hole, and still keeping it taut against the tailpiece with your right hand, leave just enough slack so that it will take only two or three revolutions of the shaft to bring it tight. You don't need to wrap it around the shaft any more than this. Now start turning the peg knob with your left hand. As soon as you've turned the shaft about 90°, pull the string back against the post in order to put a sharp kink in it to hold it against the other side of the hole. The kink will hold the string stable in the shaft hole, so now as you pull gently with your right hand you'll be holding the string taut not only against the tailpiece but against the shaft also. Don't pull the string very tight: this will cause it to distort and play out of tune. Just use enough gentle pressure to hold it in place. You must also take care not to let the kinked part of the string slip through the hole. A string that has been bent at any point between the peg and the loop or ball stands a good chance of breaking at that point, and soon.

Now just keep turning the peg until the string is tight enough that you can let go with your right hand and let it slip into its proper notch in the nut. (If you're replacing just one string, keep on tuning it up to pitch. If you're replacing all the strings at once, leave them a little loose so you can slip the bridge under them and slide it to its proper position before you tune them up to pitch.) Once the string is in tune, you can cut off the excess with cutting pliers. If you've wound carefully, holding pressure against the kink and letting the string wind downward on the shaft so that there is no tendency for it to slip off over the head of the shaft, there will be no slippage. You can cut the excess off quite close to the edge of the shaft —say, 1/4-inch—so that you won't puncture yourself by accident against a loose string end someday. If you don't have a cutter, you can just wind the excess string into a small loop. Don't let the excess string touch the headstock or other strings as this can create an annoying rattle as you play.

There are also people who wrap the string around the shaft in all kinds of strange ways, or knot it around the shaft, in order to keep it from slipping. I don't believe it's really necessary to do this. Especially knots—you practically have to be a brain surgeon to get them off when it comes time to remove the string.

Kinds of Strings

The many brands of strings are made by only a few factories. First, second, third, and fifth strings are plain steel, while the fourth has a winding of bronze, nickel, or monel alloy around a solid steel core. The most important difference between different brands of string is in diameter gauge.

Wrapping a wound string. (D'Addario Co.)

Banjo—String Gauge Chart

	GHS 150	GHS 160	GHS 170	GHS 180	Earthwood Bluegrass	Earthwood Frailing	Bell Brand 0-28½	Vega 700	Vega 730	Vega 750
1	.010	.011	.009	.011	.009	.010	.0095	.009	.010	.010
2	.012	.013	.011	.013	.011	.013	.011	.010	.012	.013
3	.014	.016	.013	.016	.013	.015	.012	.013	.016	.018
4	.022	.026	.020	.024	.020	.024	.028	.020	.023	.026
5	.010	.010	.009	.010	.009	.010	.0095	.009	.010	.010

	D'Angelico 800-L	D'Angelico 800-M	Ome Light	Ome Medium	Ernie Ball Light	Ernie Ball Medium	La Bella 730-L	La Bella 730-M	D'Addario J-60	D'Addario J-61
1	.009	.010	.009	.010	.009	.010	.010	.011	.009	.010
2	.011	.012	.011	.012	.011	.013	.012	.013	.010	.012
3	.013	.014	.013	.014	.013	.015	.014	.015	.013	.016
4	.020	.022	.020	.022	.020	.024	.019	.021	.020	.023
5	.009	.010	.009	.010	.009	.010	.010	.011	.009	.010

	D'Addario J-69	Fender 1250	Gibson G-573L	Gibson G-573	Gibson G-571	Stelling Light	Stelling Medium	Black Diamond N-40-S	Black Diamond N-625½	Black Diamond N-734½
1	.009	.009	.010	.012	.012	.010	.010	.0095	.010	.009
2	.011	.011	.011	.014	.014	.011	.012	.011	.011	.011
3	.013	.013	.012	.016	.020*	012	.014	.012	.016	.013
4	.020	.020	.018	.025	.025	.020	.022	.021	.028	.018
5	.009	.009	.010	.011	.011	.010	.010	.0095	.010	.009

*wound

String gauge is an important factor in the sound and feel of your banjo. Heavier gauge strings feel harder to play, and they tend to buzz less when the action is too low. They produce a distinctly more plunky sound, so frailers and old-timers prefer them. Some frailers go so far as to use a wound third string. However, very old frailing banjos with thin fingerboards and necks of cherry or other weak woods must not be strung too heavily. Lighter gauge strings tend to sound brighter, to provide more sustain, and to be more responsive to fingerpicks when they are used on a heavy resonator banjo, so they are the favorite strings of bluegrass players.

The Banjo-String Gauge Chart shows the comparative gauges of different brands of strings. The reason why one brand of string may sound different from another on your banjo has to do mainly with the difference in gauge since the material is basically the same from brand to brand. Sometimes you can change the *balance* of your banjo by changing string gauges. "Balance" refers to evenness of tone and volume as you go from string to string. If one of your strings seems disproportionately loud, try using a brand where that string is a lighter gauge. If one string is too soft, use a heavier gauge, or keep that string the same and go to lighter gauges on the others. However, there will also be differences in sustain and in the tone of the attack that are hard to predict, so you need to experiment some.

You'll notice from the gauge chart that first and fifth strings are the same. This means that, in a pinch, you can substitute a first for a fifth. It doesn't always work the other way around, though, because some manufacturers package a fifth string which is too short to be substituted for a first.

American manufacturers label string gauges in thousandths of an inch. A few also use metric measurements. Since we'll be switching over to the metric system one of these days, here's a metric conversion table for banjo-string gauges.

Metric Conversion Table

Inches	Millimeters
.009	.229
.010	.254
.011	.279
.012	.305
.013	.330
.014	.356
.015	.381
.016	.406
.017	.432
.018	.457
.019	.483
.020	.508
.021	.533
.022	.559
.023	.584
.024	.610
.025	.635
.026	.660

Stringing Fretless Banjos

For fretless banjos, many players prefer the soft sound of nylon strings. Gut strings are even softer, plunkier, and just plain *old*-sounding, but they're hard to come by nowadays. Gut or nylon strings are eminently suited for private or solo playing, but you will probably want to go over to steel if you play a lot with a fiddler.

Fretless banjos: (top) nineteenth-century Dobson banjo, (middle) contemporary banjo by Gary Meredith, (bottom) nineteenth-century banjo with empty fret-slots.

Strings one through four of a set of nylon (classical) guitar strings will work pretty well, with another first string to serve as your fifth. You'll have to experiment among the different brands to see which you prefer. As with steel banjo strings, there are small differences in gauge between different brands of classical guitar strings, as well as certain differences in the mass of the nylon itself. You'll probably have good luck with one of the brands that offers black nylon unwound strings. If you find that classical guitar fourth strings feel too heavy or too tight on your banjo, try a metal-wrapped nylon third string. They are made by Savarez and, in a slightly lighter gauge, by La Bella but are very rarely used by classical guitarists, so you'll probably have to special-order them. A final alternative is to do what the old-timers do, and make yourself a custom-gauged set of strings out of nylon fishing line.

Some brands of nylon strings come with ball ends. Most don't so you'll have to tie your own loop at the end of the string, or tie a knot to make your own ball.

Borrowing Guitar Strings

Someday you might be in a place where you can only find a guitar string to replace a banjo string that you have broken. You should always have extra strings, so something like this should never happen. But in case it does, here is a chart of typical guitar-string gauges.

Guitar-String Gauge Chart (First Four Strings)
Subject to variation from brand to brand

	Rock and Roll Super-Light	Extra Light	Light	Medium	Heavy
1	.009	.010	.012	.013	.014
2	.012	.014	.016	.017	.018
3	.016	.023	.025	.026	.027
4	.024	(.030)	(.032)	(.035)	(.039)

Some brands of guitar string are labelled according to precise gauge measurement, but others are simply called *light*, *medium*, etc. So you can use this chart to find an *approximate* equivalent. Just compare this chart to the Banjo-String Gauge Chart to find a close match. Remember that guitar-string manufacturers vary their designations just as banjo-string manufacturers do: "Light" may mean .011 in one brand, or .012 in another, so you may wind up with a slight mismatch. But, in an emergency, it's better than nothing.

Do You Break Strings Too Often?

You should not be frequently troubled by broken strings. If you find that you are, run down the following checklist:

1. Strings left on too long. Any string grows weak after it's been on the banjo for a long time.
2. Graceless tuning. A too-aggressive approach to turning the tuning-peg knobs can lead to broken strings.
3. Sloppy restringing. Any kinks or sharp bends that you put into the strings will create weak points that won't last long.
4. Strings too heavy. If you happen to, say, be using a rather heavy string-set you should not have any problems as long as you stay in one tuning. But if you're constantly going back and forth to a tuning where some of the strings are rather high in pitch you may be asking for trouble. For example, most manufacturers assume that in normal bluegrass tuning the second string will be at B and the first at D, but in open C tuning these strings will be at C and E respectively. Try a lighter string-set.
5. Sharp or rough bearing points. If you tend to break the same string at the same place, check the point at which it rests. The shaft of the tuning peg is one such place. A consistently broken string at this point probably indicates not a defect in the shaft itself, but your own carelessness in winding the string. Make sure that no kinks come out on the side of the shaft towards the nut.
6. Strings consistently broken at the nut. This indicates that the groove has not been filed correctly. Review the procedures for notching nuts in Chapter IX.
7. Strings consistently broken at the bridge. This indicates that the bridge is poorly notched, or that a once-good notch has been worn down. Try dressing the notch very lightly with a slim taper file, folded sandpaper, or jeweler's saw; or replace the bridge.
8. Strings consistently broken at the forward edge of a tension tailpiece. This usually indicates a sharp edge which may require beveling. Cushioning with some sort of thick tape may also work, but you'll have to replace the tape fairly often as the string wears through it.
9. Strings consistently broken at the loop or ball. This calls for an examination of the holding parts of the tailpiece. Look for jagged edges coming from wear, damage, or faulty casting or machining. You can easily dress them smooth with file or sandpaper.

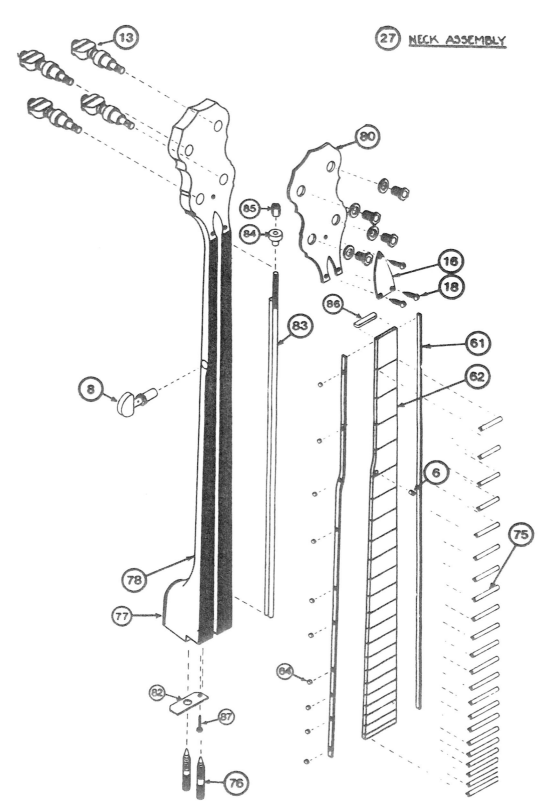

Section of factory blueprint for a modern Vega banjo. (C. F. Martin Organisation)
(13) tuning pegs, (8) fifth-string tuner, (78) necks, (77) heel plate, (82) neck shim, (87) screw for neck shim, (76) lag bolts for coordinator rods, (85) truss-rod nut, (84) truss-rod grommet, (83) two-piece truss rod, (80) headstock overlay, with washers and bushings for tuners, (16) truss-rod cover, (18) truss-rod cover screws, (86) nut, (64) position markers for binding, (61) fingerboard binding, (62) fingerboard, (6) fifth-string positioner, (75) frets.

Chapter VI
NECK, PEGHEAD, AND REINFORCING RODS

Neck and Fingerboard

People use the word *neck* unclearly. Sometimes it means the entire assembly including the neck piece *and* the fingerboard, and sometimes it means the neck piece without the fingerboard. This isn't really a problem as long as you know what you're doing, but sometimes it makes it hard to convey what you mean to someone else. So please remember that I—like everyone else—will be going back and forth between these two uses of the word *neck*.

Warping and Bowing

With the passage of time, string pressure can cause a banjo neck to pull out of shape. Careless fretting and gluing can cause this problem too, and subjecting your instrument to extremes of temperature change is no help either. The stability of the neck comes from the wood, from the fingerboard, and from various reinforcing devices which may be glued into the neck. In joints under tension, most instrument-making glues will certainly start to creep at temperatures between 150°—170°. Even a temperature of 115° could possibly cause glue to soften. The interior of a car on a hot day, an attic or crawl space, or a closet surrounded by heating ducts can easily get that hot. Careless storage is often a cause of neck distortion and many other woes.

The terminology used to describe neck distortion is not consistent within the instrument repair profession. In this book, I use the word *warp* to describe a concave curvature of the neck, and *bow* to describe a convex curvature. Others may use the words interchangeably, and speak of a forward warp or bow for concave distortion, and a reverse warp, reverse bow, or backbow to mean a convex distortion. And so on. Because different people use the words differently, you should feel no embarrassment at having to ask someone for clarification. Necks can also distort by *twisting*, where either the bass or treble side pulls higher than the other side, and by pulling into an *S-curve*, which is a roller-coaster combination of warping and bowing.

Exaggerated view of neck warp (top) and bow.

Symptoms

Bowing usually results in buzzing strings, particularly on the middle frets. Warping usually results in hard action, particularly on the middle frets. However, bowing and warping are by no means the sole causes of buzzing and action problems. See Chapter XI for a complete survey of the causes of these problems. You can detect a pretty bad case of bowing or warping very easily by looking down the fingerboard, but more subtle cases will appear only when you lay a straightedge over the frets.

Correcting Bows and Warps

Most of this chapter and a good part of the next will deal with the various ways of making and keeping the neck and fingerboard straight.

Checking the fingerboard of a classic Gibson Mastertone.

Within limits, warping, and sometimes bowing, can be corrected by loosening or tightening the adjustable reinforcing rod that is found in most banjo necks. More extreme cases may require straightening (*squaring*) the fingerboard by sanding or planing. This, in turn, means that the frets must be removed and replaced. Necks can also be corrected by heat-bending (see chapter VII).

Neck Reinforcement

Although banjo necks don't have to withstand as much string pressure as guitar necks do, they are longer, thinner, and less deep. Therefore some sort of reinforcement is desirable in order to keep the neck from distorting.

Banjo necks may have either an adjustable or nonadjustable neck reinforcement, or a combination of both. The fingerboard itself serves a reinforcing function, and it may be additionally sup-

ported by one or more additional strips of wood between itself and the neck. These thin laminations—ash and maple are among the woods favored for the job—are often dyed decorative shades of green or red. A stronger form of lamination is one that runs vertically through the neck section so that there are actually two main neck-pieces with at least one lamination down the center. The wood of such a lamination is usually cut and mounted cross-grain to the wood of the main neck sections for added strength. Ebony is favored for this application. It is often bordered by thinner strips of hardwood, perhaps dyed for decorative value.

Neck with laminated center reinforcement.

A third kind of reinforcement consists of a strip of ebony, or a bar or rod of steel, set into a long groove routed out of the neck and mounted before the fingerboard is glued over on top. Such a reinforcement must fit snugly and be glued well. Nowadays, the standard procedure is to embed the strip in epoxy putty. A poorly glued nonadjustable reinforcement of this kind can develop a serious buzz or rattle as it vibrates sympathetically to notes that are being played. Some may rattle most of the time, others only when certain notes are being played. Often it's very difficult to detect exactly where the rattle is coming from. The only real cure for this problem is to remove the fingerboard and reglue the reinforcement. On an inferior banjo where sightliness and fine craftsmanship are not at issue, you can drill through the neck from behind, up to the level of the fingerboard, and glue dowels in two or three places. It may work if you hit the right spot.

Truss Rods

Many old banjos, and almost all new ones of good quality, use one or another variation on the adjustable truss rod (also called a tension rod) system first developed and popularized by the Gibson Company. They differ completely in concept and function from nonadjustable rods. The nonadjustable rod is there simply to add strength and rigidity to the neck. The truss rod functions by setting up a pressure of its own, to oppose the pressure of the strings.

The kind of truss rod you're most likely to find in a banjo neck is about 3/16-inch diameter bar of cold-rolled steel or drill rod (carbon steel). One end is threaded to accept a hex nut. The other end has some manner of plug or anchor to keep it from rotating after it is set in the neck. It might be cast with a rectangular block at the end, be bent in an L-angle, be screwed through a rectangular block and flattened out at the other end, etc.

The rod is set into a long groove routed or dadoed down the center of the neck. On the original Gibson design, the plugged end of the rod was anchored at the heel end of the neck, while the threaded end protruded beyond the fingerboard area out through a hole in the headstock. Most other manufacturers follow this design, but you can also mount the truss rod just as easily going the opposite way, with no change in function or efficiency.

Mounting a truss rod. Note the plug at the headstock end of the rod, and the groove for the adjusting nut at the heel end of the neck.

Since the purpose of the truss rod is to oppose string pressure along the plane that produces warping, it can usually be adjusted to correct warping but not bowing. An exception is found in the case of certain unusual truss rod designs that use a double rod welded or anchored together at one end so that the two rods tighten up against each other rather than against the wood of the neck as with a conventional single rod (see diagram, page 30). This system is not often used on guitars, and even less so on banjos, but you will see it from time to time. Another unconventional design is a rod threaded at both ends, runing through nuts which are anchored to the wood at both ends. The end of the rod itself is slotted so you can turn it with a screwdriver. Turning in either direction will force the anchored nuts further apart (to correct warp) or further together (to correct bow).

The usual kind of truss rod is set well into the neck in a deep groove. It should be waxed to permit easy rotation without catching the wood. Once the rod is set, a hardwood (usually maple) overlay is glued over. This overlay should be level with the rest of the upper surface of the neck, to provide a continuous surface for gluing on the fingerboard. Since the strings exert pressure across the *top* of the neck/fingerboard structure, the truss rod must function by exerting counter-pressure along the *bottom* of the structure. It works more efficiently the more deeply it is set, even as close as 1/8-inch from the back of the neck. A truss rod with less wood above it than below it will be inefficient or even counterproductive. Someone once observed that the best truss rod would be one that was built completely outside the neck.

Some makers set their truss rods straight, while others set them curving upwards or downwards. Partisans can argue the supposed advantages of each approach far into the night, but all of these methods have one thing in common: they all do the job. Since tightening the truss rod corrects warp, many builders construct the neck with a little warp to begin with. Then they straighten the warp out with the truss rod after it is set.

In the original Gibson-style design the threaded nut end of the truss rod is set into a hollowed-out groove in the headstock and covered by a celluloid plate. Be careful with it; the celluloid is spectacularly flammable.

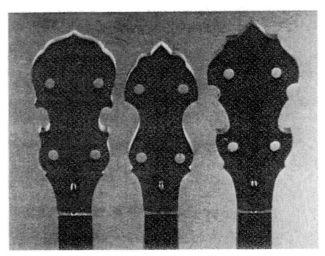

Classic peghead designs, showing truss-rod nuts. (Stewart-Macdonald Co.)

In other truss-rod designs, such as the one shown in the photo on page 33, the rod may be anchored at the headstock end with the thread down at the heel end instead. You turn the nut through a hole countersunk in the heel, and you have to remove the neck to do so. The Ome Company deliberately sets its truss rods this way in order to discourage aimless tinkering. They feel that no one will bother to take the neck off unless there is a genuine need to do so. A side benefit of this procedure is that it doesn't remove any extra wood from the point where the neck angles back to become the peghead. This is the weakest part of the neck, and it deserves all the strength it can get.

The truss rod nut is most commonly a 1/4-inch or 5/16-inch hex nut. A deep-well nut driver is the best tool to use on it, since any kind of angled socket wrench, ratchet wrench, etc. might harm the wood finish around the peghead and probably won't fit well in any case. Pliers and the like are much too awkward. Adjusting the truss rod is a sensitive job. You will also encounter variant designs that don't have hex nuts. For these you will need an allen wrench or a straight (or Phillips) screwdriver.

Adjusting the Truss Rod

Tightening the nut (clockwise) causes the rod to oppose string pressure and decreases any concavity in the neck, while loosening the nut (counterclockwise) increases the concavity. Turn the nut gently and not more than a few degrees at a time. About a quarter of a revolution is all the adjustment you'll need unless the nut has been overadjusted to begin with. Never loosen the nut past the point of snugness, since with time the neck will move back further until snugness is reached once again.

Notwithstanding the tough job that they do, truss rods are delicate creatures. They can easily be broken by careless bungling. String pressure should be kept at normal tension while loosening a truss rod, but when you tighten against a fairly serious warp it is safer to release the string tension, and perhaps apply a delicate pressure to the neck by setting the pot on the floor and holding the back of the neck against your knee. It may even be necessary to clamp it in a straightening jig (see Chapter VII). For a serious warp, it may be advisable to leave the neck in the jig for a day or two. This may straighten it out sufficiently so that the rod can be tightened up to keep it straight after the jig is removed. In really drastic cases, though, the neck could be distorted beyond the point where it can be corrected by truss-rod adjustment. In this case a more serious job of bending or of fingerboard squaring is necessary (see Chapter VII).

It takes experience to learn just what jobs can and cannot be done by adjusting the truss rod. Many inexperienced tinkerers fool with the truss rod because it's so easy to get to, but it's a dangerous business if you don't know exactly what you're doing. It's easy enough to break a truss rod, or strip the thread, or wind up with your neck in worse shape than it was to begin with.

Replacing a Truss Rod

Truss rods of the unusual double-rod design mentioned a few pages back are attached to each other rather than anchored to the neck wood. You can simply loosen the nut and pull them out. For conventional truss rods, the story is more complicated. You have to remove the fingerboard from the neck in order to get to them. Do so following the fingerboard removal procedure as described in Chapter VII. Your next task is to remove the hardwood overlay that has been glued in over the rod. It may be possible to loosen the glue by applying heat (a household clothes iron does the job) and hot water, and trying to work in a wet, hot spatula. But most likely you will have to rout it out, and cut a new overlay to replace it later on.

You can purchase a cold-rolled steel rod or the stronger carbon-steel drill rod in a hardware store, to make a new rod in the same dimensions as the original. You'll find it convenient to have tap and die if your shop does a lot of this kind of work; if not, take the rod to a machine shop to be threaded. You can recreate the plug at the anchored end of the rod by threading that end too, and then screwing it through a small steel block with a threaded hole. Let a bit of the rod come out through the hole and then hammer it flat with a ball peen hammer to keep it from coming unscrewed. If your new block is too big for the original hole, rout out the hole. If too small, plug the old hole with a piece of glued-in hardwood and rout out a new hole.

If the banjo you're working on is a modern instrument that's still in production, it may be possible for you to save yourself all this trouble by obtaining a replacement rod from the manufacturer.

Fakes and Frauds

When you're looking to buy a banjo, don't be taken in by a manufacturer's advertisement for a "steel reinforced neck." This could mean just about anything, including the insertion of an old hacksaw blade or two along the neck. Of course, this is one way to save some money on the maker's part, and if he passes the saving on to you then there's no cause for complaint. But know what you're buying when you buy.

There's one more trick you'll see, and this one is definitely sleazy. Watch out for truss rod covers on some cheapie banjos that come off to reveal: NOTHING. Such banjos usually do have a nonadjustable rod in them, but don't let the mere presence of a truss-rod cover con you into believing that there's a truss rod there. Again, it's a case of the manufacturer saving money, and if the banjo is still being sold at a fair price considering the absence of a truss rod, then so be it.

Neck and Peghead Repair

Necks can be sturdily repaired when broken close to the peghead, as can the peghead itself. The peghead may be of one piece of wood, but very often it will be of three pieces: a center piece which is an extension of the neck, and wings laminated onto either side.

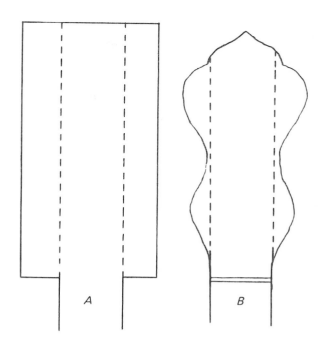

Laminated peghead (A) Rough-cut blank. (B) Peghead after shaping.

A lot of makers use this peghead design, since it doesn't waste as much wood when the neck blanks are cut. The laminations are quite secure in normal use, but sometimes one may break under impact or under shear pressure if a tuning peg hole is being reamed or drilled out. Hide glue and clamping will quickly repair the joint.

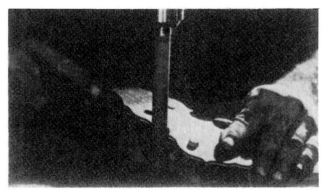

Shaping a peghead with a rotary sander mounted on a drill press. Note the template used by the craftsman to help position the peghead. (Ome. Co.)

Most pegheads have an overlay of ebony or some other attractive wood which is there mainly for decoration but which also happens to add strength to the peghead. Sometimes it's a good idea to add such an overlay to a repaired peghead that doesn't have one to begin with, in order to strengthen the joint. Some fine banjos have additional overlay on the bottom of the peghead, running down the backside of the neck well under the nut. Again, the lamination is not only decorative, but also adds a great deal of strength to this spot, which is the weakest spot on the neck and the one most likely to break when the neck suffers impact damage.

Often, the manufacturer will shape the back of the neck under the nut where it becomes the peghead with a graceful protruding knob which is called the *thumb-rest* or *handstop*. In fact it is comfortable for resting the thumb, but its real function is to provide a larger structure to support the wood grain at this crucial point.

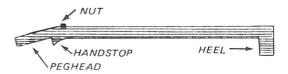

Therefore, this is the spot which you will most likely have to repair. Any repair job here is risky, and success depends upon the nature of the break. Some breaks can be repaired to last forever, but others are really touch and go. Usually a repair person will undertake to fix any break in this area to the best of his abilities, but often he may be unwilling to guarantee a particular job.

Cracks (not breaks) in the area of the nut as well as in the peghead structure itself can usually be repaired with success: simply work glue into the crack and clamp. For hairline cracks even the smallest hypodermic needle may not be able to inject sufficient glue to bond well. In that case, you can drill one or more small-diameter holes into the crack as an inlet for the glue needle.

If the peghead has been cracked off completely, success depends on the nature of the break and on how far up the neck it is. A clean squarish break across the short axis stands little chance of holding, but long jagged diagonal breaks that offer plenty of surface for gluing can usually be fixed up fine. Save any small pieces of wood that may have chipped off and try to reglue them where they belong; solid wood is better than using a lot of glue as a gap filler. Hide glue is the traditional glue for such repairs, but the choice is ultimately up to the repair person's best judgement in each individual case.

Clamping such joints is difficult, since they tend to slip but absolutely must not be permitted

to do so. Hide glue is the usual glue for this job not only for its great strength but also because of its good tack on contact. This is one job where you might want to mix the glue a little thicker than usual to increase the tack. Because of the tendency of such joints to slip during gluing, you will have to exercise your ingenuity to the utmost in developing the best combination of clamps, supporting struts, etc. Webbing clamps are often useful in this application.

You can add additional support to the peghead structure, if that is where the break is, by adding an overlay to the bottom of the peghead. Trace out a template of the peghead and use it to cut out an overlay in thin ebony or some other decorative hardwood; then glue and clamp to the

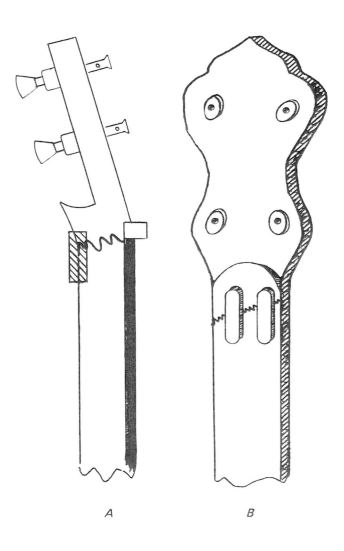

Repair of neck broken just below the peghead, using keyed-in plugs.

The plugs must be sanded flush to the neck surface after the glue has set. (A) Side view. (B) View from bottom.

back of the peghead. You'll need to cut out a section of the overlay around the handstop if the banjo has one, and bevel the edge close to where the player's thumb will ride so he won't meet a sharp rising edge as he plays.

If the break is further down, under the nut, you can reinforce the glue joint after it has set by routing out one or two grooves across the glue joint. These grooves serve as mortise joints for you to key in hardwood plugs. After their glue has set, you'll have to file and sand the keys down flush to the neck surface and refinish the area.

If gluing is absolutely hopeless, you may still be able to rescue the situation by carving a whole new peghead structure and mounting it in a V-joint or dovetail that you have cut away into the neck just below the break. You can do this only if the break is pretty close to the nut. Otherwise, the only remaining choice is to build a new neck. or put on an old neck from some other instrument. In the case of stock banjos still in production, you can of course get a new factory neck.

Preliminary factory shaping of a neck blank on a rotary sander. (Ome. Co.)

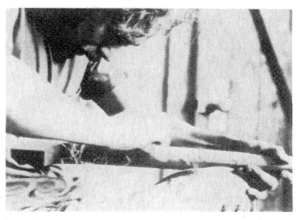

Hand-planing a neck to its final shape. (Ome Co.)

Chapter VII
FINGERBOARD, FRETS, AND NECK STRAIGHTENING

As you sight down the fingerboard of your instrument, looking down over the left or right side of the nut towards the bridge, you may notice that the fingerboard is not exactly straight and that the tops of the frets are not exactly level with each other. A very small degree of this deviation from absolute straightness is desirable. To judge the point at which it becomes undesirable requires a very experienced eye. Indeed, the real test is not by eye at all, but by sound and feel: the strings should not buzz against the frets. Different players have different touches and different standards of comfort, so that an instrument may buzz under one player's fingers but not under another's. Your own banjo, when strung with the kind of strings you normally use, should not buzz at loud volume--the level of consistent loudness that is your *own* idea of loud playing. If you go one step louder than this, and the strings begin to buzz, then you're in good shape. Your banjo is telling you that you've gotten the strings down as close to the fingerboard as they need to be, and no further.

Each player must find his own standards of action. If you play hard, heavy, and close to maximum volume all the time, then you need to worry more about buzzing than you would if you played very lightly all the time, and you will have to learn to like a slightly higher action. If you hate high action but like to play loud now and then, you may even decide that you can live with a little bit of buzzing. Of course, a perfectly set up banjo should have pretty easy action and still not buzz at all, but the fact of life is that buzzes do appear. Sometimes they'll come and go. If you live in a climate with seasonal differences in humidity, for example, you can expect your instrument to sound and feel very different from one season to the next as the wood of the neck and fingerboard expands and contracts from the moisture in the air. You may decide that living with some buzzing during the summer months is easier than having to readjust your banjo every other season.

But there are other causes of buzzing that you shouldn't dismiss so lightly Warping, bowing, and other forms of neck distortion can and should be rectified. If truss-rod adjustment, as discussed in the preceding chapter, is not sufficient, then you must do more serious work on the neck and fingerboard.

Fingerboard Relief

No fingerboard should be perfectly straight, for the simple reason that a plucked string does not vibrate in a straight line, but rather in an arc. Therefore a plucked open string will buzz against the lower frets if the action is as low as it should be and the neck is perfectly straight. To avoid this kind of buzzing, most makers build a slight deliberate warp into the fingerboard. If this isn't done, the only other way to avoid this buzz would be to raise the nut and bridge, leading to unnecessarily high action and making the banjo feel rather stiff to play. The built-in curvature designed to eliminate this buzzing problem is called *fingerboard relief*. The problem is most pronounced on the lower frets and the open string, since the arc of the vibrating string grows smaller as you move up the fingerboard, and the angle of the string up towards the bridge grows relatively greater. Therefore, fingerboard relief is most important in reference to the first few frets.

The fingerboard relief on a banjo is so small that it might be hard to see. It appears as a dip across the lower frets as you sight down the fingerboard, and perhaps a slight hump down towards where the heel begins.

Frets

Frets are available from instrument supply houses in the form of large coiled strips. It is also possible to buy fretwire in shorter precut lengths, but this is less economical and you lose the convenience of being able to work with a long edge extended over the side of the fingerboard for you to hold onto while you're setting the fret. Fretwire is available in a number of sizes and variations. The smaller sizes of fretwire are generally used on banjos, but some players prefer the wider, guitar-size frets. The best material for fretwire is the nickel alloy known as *nickel silver* or *German silver* due to its silvery appearance (it actually has no silver content). Brass wire is also available, and was often used on banjos in the past. It is softer than nickel silver, and wears down faster.

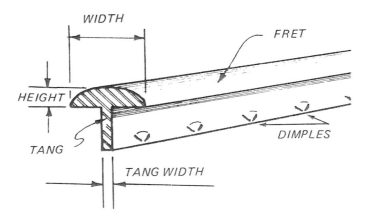

The principle dimensions of a fret. (H. Kamimoto)

The diagram above shows the terminology used to describe the different parts of the fret. The dimples are small protrusions found at about 1/8-inch intervals that have the job of holding the fret firmly in the wood of the fingerboard. They are sometimes called *studs* or *serrations*.

Some old banjos still have their original, old-fashioned, "square" fretwire; a simple rectangular shape that is seated directly into the wood without benefit of tang or dimple. These frets tend to rise now and then and have to be redriven with a plastic-tipped mallet. The square tops feel a bit jagged under the fingers and it's difficult to make smooth slides, so most players like to have them rounded off a bit. The procedure is called *crowning*. Simply dress the fret along its length with a fret file of the correct size. Occasionally a specialist in reconstructing old instruments will custom-order a batch of old-style fretwire from a mill, but I know of no one at present who can furnish a supply. Inquiries within the parts-supply trade at a given time may turn up a batch. Otherwise, it may be necessary to replace an old-style fret with a new-style one. Occasionally a collector will demand than an old banjo be refretted with its original-style frets, but the new-style frets hold better and should be used for a complete refretting whenever possible.

Dressing Frets

With time, frets become worn down and grooved in those places that receive the most use. *Dressing* or *milling* the frets may put off the time that the first fret must be replaced. For this procedure, a large, smooth *mill file* is used to remove only the slightest amount of metal from the tops of the frets, sufficient to level them. A second going-over with 150-grit sandpaper in a sanding block will smooth down the frets. For a slight job of dressing, the sandpaper alone may be sufficient. The kind of sanding block to use for this job is the long, thin *sanding plane* or *sandpaper file* used in auto body work and available from an auto supply shop. The mill file should have its tang cut off so as not to get in the way, and most repair persons find the file easier to use if it is mounted on a wood-block holder.

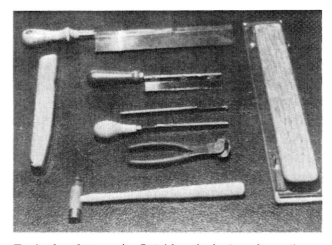

Tools for fret work. Outside, clockwise: dovetail saw, sanding file, mallet, fret files mounted on wood block. Inside, top to bottom: hobbyist's saw, fret files, and end nippers with edge ground flat. In addition, a dentist's pick is a useful tool for cleaning wood or glue chips out of fret-slots.

Since you will need space to move the file and sander back and forth across the frets, you'll have to remove the nut (and perhaps the tuners) temporarily when doing fret work.

Milling the frets will have flattened them out a bit, so you'll want to shape up the crowns with a *fret file*. Painstaking work with a small *three-cornered* or *safe-edge file* will also do the job. Take care to avoid messing up the fingerboard with the edges of the file. Some fret files come with rather sharp edges, but you can bevel these yourself—on a stone, with another file, etc.—in order to minimize danger to the fingerboard. If you want to play it really safe, cover the wood right up to the edge of the fret with thick masking tape. Once the frets have been crowned, you can run your fingers over them to test for rough spots and do any final touching-up with a fine grade of sandpaper. Remember that a little extra metal will be coming off the frets in the final crowning and smoothing, so don't take too much off with the mill file at first.

Now run your finger along the edges of the fingerboard to check for any protruding jagged edges of frets. Dressing may leave a jagged edge, or a little edge may protrude on older instruments as the fingerboard wood shrinks slightly over the years. Protruding frets are very uncomfortable for the player. The edges should be finished at about a 45° angle, beveling delicately with a small three-cornered file or a mill file mounted at a 45° angle in a wood block. Finally, smooth down the edges with a fine grit of sandpaper and clean off the whole fingerboard with 0000-grade steel wool and some lemon oil.

Fret milling is a procedure that must be carried out for all of the frets across the span of the fingerboard. Sometimes you can successfully dress a single worn fret, but usually that fret will wind up too low in relation to the nut or adjacent frets and you'll have a buzzing problem. If just a single fret or two is damaged, the best bet is to replace it.

Refretting

After a certain amount of fret milling, there will be no more fret to mill. At this point, it's time to replace the frets. Often it will not be necessary to replace all the frets.

The first step in refretting is to pull the old frets. The fingerboard will compress slightly when the frets are removed, and will bow back when the frets are replaced. In fact, there is a technique for putting a deliberate bow in a neck by replacing the old frets with new ones of a slightly larger tang-size.

The preferred tool for pulling frets is an *end-nipper* (*end-cutting pliers*) on which the edges that come in contact with the fingerboard have been ground flat in order to allow the cutting edge to fit neatly under the sides of the fret. This helps to keep from chipping the fingerboard wood as the fret comes out. Ebony almost always chips a little. You can replace large chips immediately if you keep some cyanoacrylate glue handy, since it bonds on contact. Any other bad chips can be filled in at the end of the job using a mix-

ture of ebony dust (or rosewood dust for a rosewood fingerboard) and epoxy which is then sanded smooth after the glue cures.

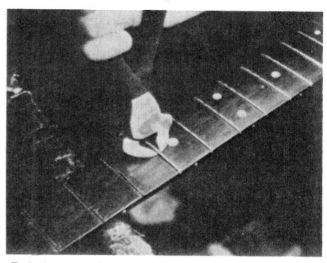

End nippers used to pull frets, in this case on a guitar. In order to allow the cutting edges to fit under the fret crown and grasp it firmly without damaging the fingerboard wood, the side of the end nippers shown in contact with the fingerboard must be ground flat. (H. Kamimoto)

Use the nippers to pull the frets by working from one end of the fret to the other, pulling up a little bit at a time. Only after the whole fret has been moved a little in this way should you begin to pull it completely out, again working from one end of the fret to the other.

This procedure will work only for frets that have been driven directly into the wood in the traditional manner. In recent years it has become fashionable to use glue—usually epoxy—to seat the fret in its slot. If this is the way the instrument you're working on has been fretted, you'll pull half the wood off the fingerboard trying to get the frets out with the nippers. You first have to heat the frets to loosen the glue. Use a soldering iron, moving across the fret from one end to the other in several sections, and pulling up a section at a time with the nippers. You might also try a clothing iron, but with epoxy this may not get the frets hot enough to make the glue creep. I know of one instance where a repairman charred the fingerboard with an iron before he could get the epoxy loose. Fortunately, the board needed dressing anyway, so it was easy to sand off the charred part.

If the instrument you're working on has a bound fingerboard, you needn't remove the binding in order to remove the frets. However, when you refret, you'll have to take the extra trouble of cutting the frets precisely to size before you drive them. Use calipers to take the measurement inside the binding. You'll have to do this fret by fret, since some fingerboards get slightly wider as they approach the heel. For storing newly cut frets, or old ones that have been removed and are being kept in reserve, you can take a longish block of wood and drill out twenty-two holes in it, one for each fret.

Binding rarely has to be removed for a simple fret job. When it does have to come off, as for extensive fingerboard dressing, pry it gently loose with a *hobbyist's knife*, and reserve it for regluing with plastic cement and clamping with a web clamp. Be careful where you keep any loose binding material, since it's highly flammable. Some makers finish their banjos with a continuous layer of finish that covers the wood and also overlaps the binding. If this is the case, you'll have to scrape the finish layer off the binding before you remove it. Otherwise you'll pull chips of finish off the wood along with the binding.

Squaring the Fingerboard

If the fingerboard needs dressing for straightness, now is the time. Judging what needs to be done now that the strings and frets are off takes an experienced eye. With the truss rod still adjusted to oppose the tension of the strings which are no longer on, and with the fingerboard compressing slightly into the slots of the frets which are no longer on, the neck will have more of a warp to it than it would under normal playing circumstances. You might back off the truss rod a little, and tighten it up again later.

For leveling the board, use a sanding plane with about 180 grit paper. If there are large inlay surfaces, you may have to use a finer paper to minimize scratching. If the job is a drastic one, with serious humps and irregularities in the board, you can use a razor-sharp block plane if there are no inlays.

Once the board is pretty well squared off, with some allowance for string relief, you can smooth it down with successively finer sandings. Do the last stages by hand, not with the sanding plane.

This whole procedure is a very delicate one, and one that calls for experienced judgment. You have to gauge the effect of many interrelated variables: truss-rod pressure, string pressure, fingerboard relief, bridge and nut height, fret height, and the angle of the neck to the pot.

Heat-Straightening a Warped or Bowed Neck

You can usually correct a simple and not-too-drastic warp or bow, if it's not complicated by an S-curve or sideways twist, without having to pull the frets and square the fingerboard. To do this, heat the neck and clamp it in a *straightening jig* (described below).

This procedure works only within limits. It's an especially good way to do a little straightening-out on a neck that doesn't have an adjustable truss rod. It takes experienced judgment to determine whether you can get away with heat-straightening, or whether squaring is called for. If in doubt, try heat-straightening first; it's by far the simpler procedure. However, it also takes experience to determine just how much heat and pressure a given job requires.

Sometimes it's a good idea to use the straightening-jig set-up for warped necks when you're tightening up a truss rod on a hard-to-turn or fairly drastic job. In this case, don't apply heat; just clamp on the jig to help the truss rod do its work.

To construct the jig, you'll need a couple of wood shims big enough to fit over the fingerboard in between the frets. Over these will sit a platen consisting of a good strong hardwood block about two inches wide by eighteen inches or so long—long enough to cover most of the span of the fingerboard. It must be rigid enough not to bend under clamping pressure, which usually means a thickness of not less than two inches, and maybe more. If necessary, you can glue several thinner layers together to build up a rigid enough block.

To begin with, heat the neck slowly, fingerboard down, over a *spirit lamp*. A half-hour should be more than necessary. You can tell when the neck is hot enough when it has been heated through from the fingerboard and the back of the neck is pretty warm. Some repair persons use infra-red heat lamps instead of—or in addition to—the spirit lamp.

While the neck is heating, get the jig ready. You'll need the shims and platen, two C-clamps, and some padding material (leather-faced wood chocks, etc.) to cushion the neck from the clamps.

To correct a warp, place the shims towards the high and low ends of the neck and clamp at the middle. Two clamps will give a more even distribution of pressure over the warp area than one will.

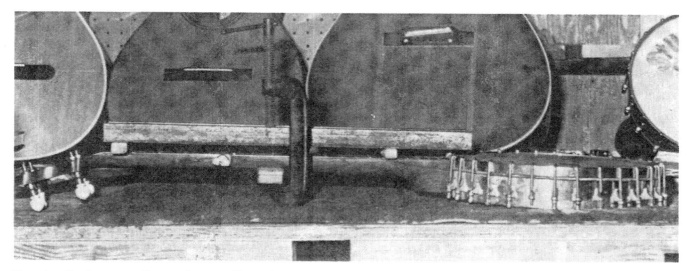

Clamping jig for correcting neck warp. Two clamps instead of one may be used if the warp covers a long section of the neck.

To correct a bow, set the shims towards the middle of the neck—at the middle of the bowed area. (Using two shims will distribute pressure more evenly than one, but if you use two don't set them too far apart.) Then clamp at the high and low ends of the neck.

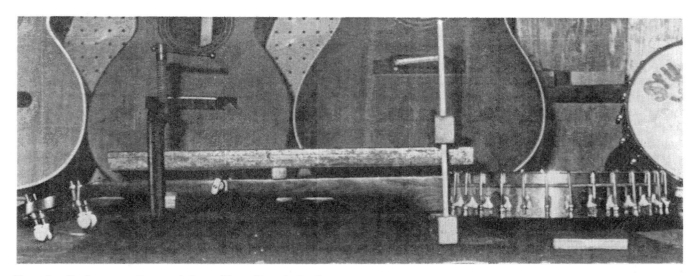

Clamping jig for correcting neck bow. Two shims instead of one may be used if the bow covers a long section of the neck.

Check the neck from time to time, especially during the crucial first few minutes, and make any changes in clamping pressure that seem necessary. Remember that you need to overcompensate a little in clamping, since the neck will spring slightly back when you release the jig. Unclamp it once the neck has cooled completely. You may discover that you have to repeat the procedure, or that you need to do a little fret-dressing to eliminate some new buzzes.

Replacing the Frets

It's easier to work with long pieces of fretwire so you can get a good hold of them. Use a plastic-headed mallet. Drive the ends in first, then work in towards the center. The fret must be perfectly aligned and perpendicularly seated. If a blow lands askew and bends the fretwire, pull it and start with a new section. You can rough-cut the end of the fret with nippers or a file. It is then ready for final dressing, as described in the preceding section, "Refretting."

Driving frets. (Ome Co.)

It has recently become fashionable to use Don Teeter's method (see bibliography) of seating the frets in epoxy. To do this, you must rout out the fret slot a bit wider than the tang (about .005-inch wider) with the Dremel tool fitted with a dental burr. Make sure that the fingerboard around the fret slots is protected from epoxy squeeze-out with masking tape. Once the frets are driven, they must be clamped in a jig consisting of a straight board laid across the frets and held by three or four cushioned C-clamps. (Teeter describes a more complicated jig in his book, but it's for oval guitar fingerboards. Banjo fingerboards are flat.)

Seating the fret in epoxy has a few advantages: the fret won't pop up the way driven frets sometimes do, and the fret can be seated without chipping the fingerboard. This can be important on very old and brittle fingerboards that tend to chip and crack badly. The epoxy method also makes sense on old fingerboards where the fret slots have become so wide that you'd otherwise have to use oversize frets. The great disadvantage is that removing epoxied-in frets is a tremendous job (see section, "Refretting"). As a result, many repair persons find the epoxy method attractive only in special cases; for example, on a very old and brittle ebony fingerboard that might just about fall to pieces if the frets were conventionally driven—or on an instrument where they have reason to believe that this fret job, for whatever reason, will be the last. In any case, if you are a professional repair person and do this or *any* job with epoxy, be sure to tell your customer so that he can warn the next repair person who works on the instrument that extra care will have to be taken in loosening the glue joints.

Replacing a Fingerboard

Occasionally a fingerboard becomes so worn, damaged, or distorted that the less drastic remedies of filling in pits with a mixture of wood dust and epoxy, or of squaring and refretting, just won't work anymore. Getting a broken truss rod out and replacing it is another reason for removing a fingerboard, but on such a job you'll be replacing the original fingerboard rather than cutting a new one.

Begin by knocking off the nut (see chapter IX). You'll also have to remove the binding if the fingerboard is a bound one. Do this by slipping in a thin-bladed hobbyist's knife.

Then you need to get the glue loose. Do this by inverting the fingerboard over a spirit lamp, or use a clothing iron laid over the frets. You can protect the bottom of the iron from rosewood oil or ebony stain by using aluminum foil or a thin sheet metal as a buffer. Once the glue has softened, you can work in a heated knife or spatula moistened in hot water to gently pry the board off the neck. Since you'll be heating in sections, you'll be prying in sections also. Doing the job under infrared heat lamps may help a little, but heat from the lamps alone will probably not be sufficient. Needless to say, you should be doing all this after you have first loosened the rim—stick and removed the neck from the pot.

Once the board is off, inspect the neck surface and sand it flush, removing patches of old glue and any slivers of ebony or rosewood that may have remained. If you're going to be replacing the original fingerboard, try to pry or knock off any larger slivers intact so you can glue them back to the underside of the board. This is one job where cyanoacrylate glue is convenient.

You're now ready to glue down the new fingerboard. You may have been able to purchase a precut standard-model board from the factory or from a supplier, or you may have cut your own board from a rough blank according to the procedures described in the next section.

The most difficult part of replacing a fingerboard is aligning it precisely with the neck, since it tends to slip around. Repairmen use aliphatic resin, polyvinyl resin, or hide glue for this job depending on preference. Of the three, hide glue has the best tack and will slip least. For a new fingerboard, you can drill a few small holes in places where there will eventually be inlays and mount positioning studs made of cut-down finishing nails. Align the neck and fingerboard, clamp them tightly together, and drill through the fingerboard and just enough into the neck to hold the stud. Pull them when the glue has set. When replacing an original fingerboard, you can pull two or three frets and drill for the studs through the fret slots. Then you'll have to replace the frets after the studs have been pulled.

Before you glue, prepare the edges of the neck with masking tape to protect the finish from squeeze-out. Clamp down the new board with three or four C-clamps bearing on a wood caul resting over the entire length of the fingerboard. You'll have to protect the bottom of the neck from clamp pressure. The best cushion is a wood block with one concave surface for the neck to rest in, softened by an additional layer of felt, leather, etc. As with all glue jobs, run through a glueless dress rehearsal of the whole clamping process just to see how things line up.

Once the clamps are screwed down remove the glue squeeze-out. When the glue has set, you're ready for final dressing and refretting if necessary. Then comes inlaying, mounting the fifth-string holder and nut, and replacing the binding.

Cutting a Fingerboard

Rough-cut ebony or rosewood neck blanks are easily available from suppliers. You can use

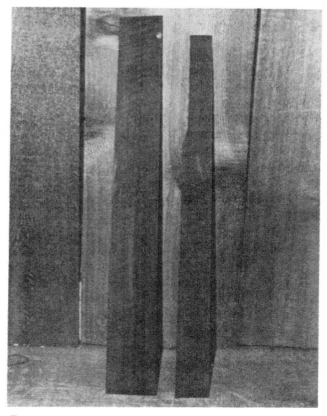

Fingerboards. (left) rough-cut blank, (right) fingerboard shaped and slotted.

the original fingerboard as a template for cutting them to precise size. A hand-held power sander does a quick job of reducing the board to the desired thickness if you have a good touch for evenness, but in any case finish off the job by hand-sanding with a sanding file. In the absence of a power sander, you might use a block plane for the earlier rough stages of reducing the board if you're going to be taking a lot of wood off. The final smoothing, including the removal of a bit more wood, will take place in the last dressing of the board after it has been glued to the neck.

Now it's time to cut the fret-slots. If the original fingerboard has been accurately fretted (as is almost certainly the case) you can simply copy its fret spacing. Or you can copy the fingerboard of another banjo of the identical dimension. Otherwise you'll have to compute the proper spacing on your own, following the procedures given in the section, "Measuring for Fret Placement."

Mark the fret locations clearly in fine pencil or with a scribe, using a straightedge. Whether you need to mark the top or side of the board depends on what part of the board will be visible to you, which depends on whether you'll be using a handsaw or table saw. Use a blade that will cut the slot to the size of the tang you'll be using. The slot should be wide enough that a hefty press with hand pressure will amost be sufficient to seat the fret. It shouldn't really be necessary on a new fingerboard to have to seat the frets in epoxy. If you happen to like this method anyway, then cut the slots about .005-inch wider than the tang size.

Cut the fret-slots on a table saw with a *hollow-ground blade*, or by hand with a *dovetail saw*. The slots must be absolutely parallel to each other and perpendicular to the side of the fingerboard, so use an *index* to guide the fingerboard over the saw table, or hold the dovetail saw in a *fence*. You can set the power saw blade to the right height for the fret tang. You'll have to determine the depth of the slots freehand when using the dovetail saw, unless you have the kind of fence that lets you determine the depth of the cut. Such a fence is a good investment.

Now you're ready to mount the fingerboard. Drive the frets, replace the binding, etc. after the board is glued to the neck.

Partial Replacement of a Fingerboard

If only part of a fingerboard is damaged, it can be partially replaced. This procedure should be followed advisedly, since it can be difficult to get fingerboard woods to match and because you wind up with a two-piece fingerboard that doesn't add as much strength to the neck as a one-piece fingerboard does. It does save a lot of trouble on instruments where you would have to replace a fancy inlay job, and it can save money on a cheap banjo where a complete fingerboard replacement would barely be worth the cost.

The job is easy enough. Pull the fret or frets that comprise the boundary of the damaged area and saw the fingerboard through the fret–slots down to the level of the neck. Remove the nut and binding, if necessary. Then remove the damaged portion of the fingerboard and replace it with a new section cut from a fingerboard blank.

Measuring for Fret Placement.

You will usually be able to position the frets on a new fingerboard by copying the old fingerboard, or the fingerboard of another banjo of the same scale-length. (*Scale*, you'll remember from Chapter III, is the word used to describe the total length of the vibrating part of the string between nut and bridge, with the 12th fret located at the midpoint.)

If the original fingerboard has not been accurately fretted, or if the scale length is unusual and you can't find another model to copy, then you'll have to compute the fret spacing yourself.

Today's banjos, and most of yesterday's have twenty-two frets. The Pete Seeger style long-neck banjo has an extra-long neck with three extra frets at the low end. (It is usually tuned a minor third low and played with a capo at the 3rd fret.) Many old-time banjos were made with fewer than twenty-two frets, but without the neck being shortened proportionally: the maker simply didn't bother to put in the highest five frets or so, leaving a blank space at the high end of the fingerboard. Hardly anyone feels an overwhelming need to play up there anyway, particularly in old-time style. The scale-length of most banjos is between 26 and 26½ inches, though it could be as long as 27 inches and a few are as short as 25 inches.

You will find it safest and most convenient to lay out the fret-spacing on a cardboard or sheet-metal template before you mark it out on the actual fingerboard. That way you can double-check your calculations, and reserve the template for future projects. Confirm that the 12th fret is in fact at the halfway point, the 5th fret 1/4 of the way up the first half, and the 17th fret 1/4 of the way up the second half. Check visually to make sure that the distance between frets grows consistently smaller.

To compute fret-spacing exactly, start with the desired scale-length and divide by 17.817.

Different kinds of banjos have different numbers of frets. (top) a short-neck Stewart-Macdonald *banjorine* with only seventeen frets, (bottom) a custom Great Lakes banjo by Mark Grube, with the standard twenty-two frets. (Also see photos on page 48 and 94.)

This gives the distance to the 1st fret. Now subtract that distance from the total scale-length and divide again by 17.817 to find the distance to the second fret. And so on, always dividing the total *remaining* length by 17.817. Needless to say, the whole operation is much simpler if you use a pocket calculator.

Another way to lay out the fret-spacing is to construct a template with ruler and compass. Hideo Kamimoto describes the procedure as follows in his excellent book, *Complete Guitar Repair*, reprinted with the kind permission of Oak Publications. Since Kamimoto is talking about guitars, he describes scale as the distance between nut and *saddle*; just substitute the word *bridge* to talk about banjos.

You can construct a scale geometrically rather than by cranking out mind-numbing fractions with pencil and paper. On a heavy sheet of paper, or on a thin sheet of aluminum or brass if the scale is to be kept for future use, draw a straight line the exact length of the scale. Calculate the distance to the first fret and with a pair of dividers mark out this distance. Now swing the dividers around, pivoting around the nut (or zero feet) so that a quarter arc is described which intersects a perpendicular drawn up from the nut. From this intersection draw a straight line down to the other end of the scale (the saddle). A perpendicular drawn at the first fret will intersect the tangent line and will automatically give the distance between the first fret and the second. Adjust the dividers at the first fret to the distance between the tangent and base line and draw an arc to the base line; this will give you the distance to the second fret. Continue in the same fashion for the remaining frets.

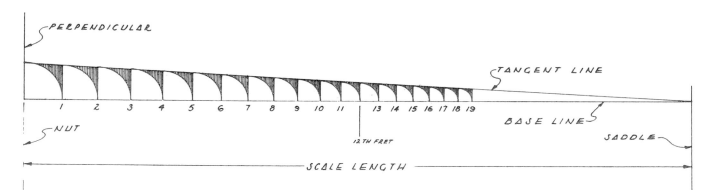

LAYING OUT A SCALE GEOMETRICALLY

1. DETERMINE SCALE LENGTH.
2. CALCULATE DISTANCE TO FIRST FRET.
3. SET COMPASS TO FIRST FRET DISTANCE AND SCRIBE ARC FROM BASE LINE TO PERPENDICULAR.
4. DRAW TANGENT LINE.
5. DRAW PERPENDICULAR AT 1ST FRET DISTANCE.
6. RESET COMPASS TO DISTANCE FROM 1. TO TANGENT AND SCRIBE ARC.
7. CONTINUE, DRAWING PERPENDICULAR LINES AT EACH FRET POSITION AND SCRIBING ARCS TO DETERMINE THE NEXT FRET POSITION.
8. THE 12TH FRET SHOULD BE EXACTLY AT THE MIDPOINT OF THE SCALE LENGTH.

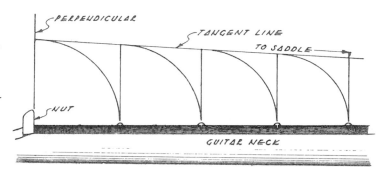

Fretless-Banjo Fingerboards

The usual fretless-banjo fingerboard is just like any other rosewood or ebony fingerboard, except that it has no frets. Other woods can also

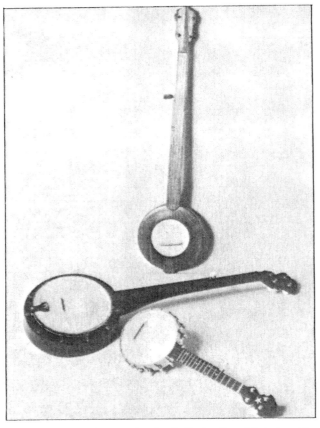

(top) a modern fretless banjo, built in the old style without tension hoop, (middle) a nineteenth-century fretless banjo bearing a Dobson Bros. patent, (bottom) a fifteen-fret S.S. Stewart *piccolo banjo* from the early part of this century.

be used. I've never seen a maple fingerboard on a banjo, but it seems to me it would work well. Telecaster guitars with maple fingerboards have a wonderful hard feel to them and the smoothest-playing fretless banjo I've ever had the pleasure to hold in my hands had a formica fingerboard. Now I know this idea will rankle some (since formica is pure plastic and definitely unorganic), but it sure does give you a smooth, hard playing surface.

For converting from a standard to a fretless banjo there's a good trick that the old-timers in the mountains used to use a lot to save the trouble of putting on a new fingerboard. You simply encase the fingerboard in a sheet-metal, sheath, folded about 1/4-inch—the depth of the fingerboard—over the sides of the neck. Assuming that you're using a fairly non-descript banjo, you can fix it into the edges of the fingerboard with a few small nails. As a rule people play the fretless banjo only in the lower positions, so the sheath doesn't have to cover more than the first five or seven frets. The metal should be fairly thick so that it won't scallop down between the frets. You could also simply pull the frets. I've seen fretless sheaths made of copper, brass, nickel silver and sheet steel.

Sheath-style nickel-silver fingerboard extender on an old Dobson. On some fretless banjos, the entire fingerboard is covered by such a sheath.

Another way to fix up a rather makeshift fretless banjo is simply to pull the frets out of a standard one. This leaves you with a rather unsightly fingerboard that's not at all smooth to play on, and you'll muff some notes if you finger them over the fret-slots, but basically the idea will work. Then, at your leisure, you can fill in the fret-slots with hardwood strips flush to the fingerboard surface. Using a light-colored hardwood will give you a rather decorative neck that will probably be more visually attractive than one where you attempt to match the old fingerboard; most likely you won't get a good enough match. Every so often you'll come across a beautiful old fretless banjo with ivory "frets" set flush to the fingerboard.

Chapter VIII
RIM-RODS AND NECK-ANGLE

The function of the various devices known as *rim-rods, rim-sticks,* or *coordinator rods* is to attach the neck to the rim. A snug and stable fit is essential for good banjo sound, since the neck performs the secondary acoustic function of absorbing sound impulses at the nut, as well as through the fingerboard, and transmitting them back to the rim. Besides, a poorly set neck will wobble as you play, causing the strings to stretch and playing havoc with intonation. The rim-stick also provides stiffness and support across the diameter of the rim itself.

Neck Angle

Most rim-stick configurations can be altered to slightly raise or lower the angle at which the neck abuts the rim. This angle is one of the factors that determines the height and consistency of the action over the length of the fingerboard. The strings should be almost parallel to the fingerboard although the specific dimensions may vary according to the player's preference and the nature of the banjo itself. Taking my own banjo as an example, string height is 3/64-inch above the first fret, rising only to 5/64-inch at the 12th fret and 6/64-inch at the 22nd fret. The degree of the angle between string and neck can be changed by manipulating the rim-stick. However, first make sure that the undesirable string-angle is not due to a bridge of the wrong height. Sometimes you will find a banjo that has been so carelessly set up that changing both the bridge-height and the neck-angle is necessary. You may have to experiment a bit in order to sort out these two variables.

Lag bolts set into the neck-heel. The metal coordinator rods will screw onto the lag bolts from inside the rim.

Shims

The neck-angle can also be altered by inserting a *shim-strip* of wood veneer, celluloid pickguard material, etc. between the end of the fingerboard and the tension hoop. Shimming at this point has the effect of setting the neck-angle further back. It is also possible on many banjos to find a way to get a shim between the heel and the rim, which has the effect of bringing the neck a little forward. You'll need to loosen the rim-stick in order to get the neck a little loose to slip in the shim, but on very few banjos will you have to take the neck completely off.

Shimming can be done instead of or in addition to rim-stick adjustment. Again, it takes experimentation or an experienced eye to judge the relative effects of these two variables.

Lag Bolts

There are several kinds of metal rim-stick design. Most of them depend on *lag bolts* for attaching the neck to the rest of the rim-stick assembly. A lag bolt is a bolt threaded at one end like a wood screw and at the other end to accept a nut.

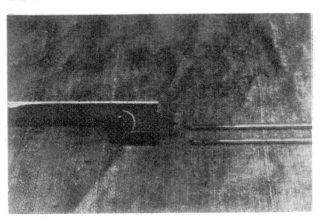

On some banjos, particularly modern kit banjos, the neck is simply attached to the rim with two lag bolts running from the heel of the neck through holes in the rim, and held on with hex nuts tightened against the inside of the rim. This is a relatively poor way to attach the neck, since it offers little in the way of stability and support. It works, though, and it's one way to save a little money. Since there is no real rim-stick in this design, the only way to adjust neck-angle is by shimming or by shaving the wood of the heel where it abuts the rim.

Coordinator Rods

Most modern banjos are constructed with one or another variation on the metal *coordinator-rod* system developed by the Gibson company. The basic idea is that a rod runs across the diameter of the rim, attached to a lag bolt at the heel end and to a screw or hex nut at the tailpiece end. This is the lower of the two rods when there are two; some manufacturers use only one. The upper rod, if there is one, lends additional stability to the neck. A one-rod neck is liable to be a little wobbly after adjustment, in which case you must insert a shim.

The classic Gibson coordinator rod setup. Note the custom heel carving.

The rod itself is of a fixed length, and must be held steady during adjustment. By turning the outside hex nut, however, you can pull the neck tighter or let it become looser against the rim.

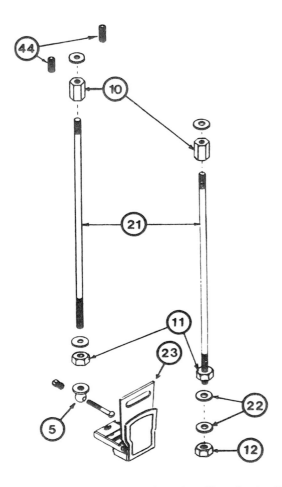

Section of factory blueprint of modern Vega banjo. The rod on the right is actually the lower rod. (C.F. Martin Organisation)
(44) lag bolts, (10) inside hex nuts, (21) coordinator rods, (11) inside hex nuts, (5) tailpiece bracket shoe, (22) rim washers, (12) outside hex nut.

Adjusting Coordinator Rods

Bear in mind that you can adjust action and neck-angle only within small limits with the coordinator rod, or with any other kind of rim-stick for that matter. Figure an adjustment of 1/16-inch in action height or two revolutions of the adjusting nut, as the upper limit, unless you're correcting a banjo that was badly out of kilter to begin with. You don't want to make too great an adjustment because turning the nut will stretch or compress the diameter of the rim. Undue pressure is bad for the structural integrity of the rim, seeing as it consists of laminations held together by glue joints. Even worse, you wind up putting the rim out of round, leading to poor fit of the tone ring and tension hoop—in other words, to the general disintegration of the whole pot structure.

Raising and Lowering Neck-Angle with Coordinator Rods

Some banjos have two coordinator rods, an upper and lower; some have just one. Some have a combination of single coordinator rod plus hex nut and lag bolt.

The lower coordinator rod is the important one for adjusting neck-angle. If your banjo has an upper coordinator rod, loosen the hex nuts on the inside of the rim and tighten them up again after the lower rod is adjusted. If it has a lag bolt, loosen the hex nut and then tighten it up again after the lower rod is adjusted. The purpose of the upper coordinator rod, or of the lag bolt and hex nut, is to add additional stability.

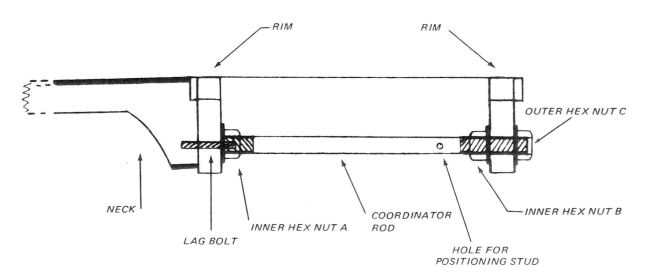

Adjustable (bottom-type) coordinator rod.

The diagram above represents an idealized coordinator-rod setup. You'll see a total of three hex nuts. Nut A tightens against the rim near the neck, nut B against the opposite side. Some banjos have both these nuts, others have just one or the other.

The third hex nut (nut C) is on the outside of the rim, below the tailpiece bracket. By tightening this nut, you pull the coordinator rod further through its hole in the rim. This in turn compresses the rim and draws the heel back against the rim, bringing back the angle of the neck. Some banjos have a slot-screw instead of a hex nut.

To alter the neck-angle with the coordinator rod, follow this procedure.

1. Loosen the nuts on the upper rod (or the upper lag bolt, if there is one). Tighten them up again after the lower rod is adjusted. You'll notice that both the upper and lower rods have a small hole in them. Insert a nail or stud through this hole to keep the rod from moving as you adjust the nuts.

2. Loosen the inside nuts (nuts A and/or B) on the lower rod. Then tighten up the outside nut (nut C) to bring back the neck-angle, or loosen it to bring the neck-angle up. Then check to see that the end of the coordinator rod near the neck is flush to the inside of the rim. If not, turn the rod (using the nail through the hole) to bring it flush. Hold the outside nut to keep it from turning along with the rod. Then tighten up the inside nuts.

To remove the neck completely, take down all the nuts and use the nail through the rod-hole to unscrew the rod from its lag bolts.

Anchored Lag Bolts

On some banjos, particularly older Gibsons, the lower lag bolt is anchored into place instead of screwing in on a wood-screw thread.

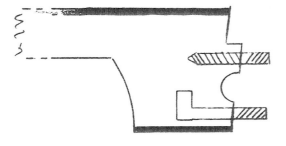

Threaded (top) and anchored (bottom) lag bolts.

To anchor the lag bolt, the maker has routed out the heel from the underside, mounted the bolt in its routed-out groove, and then covered up the groove by gluing in a hardwood overlay. The underside of the heel is then covered with a decorative heel plate, so that the job is impossible to detect from underneath. It may also be difficult to see the joint from the butt end of the heel, so the only way that you can guess that the lag bolt is anchored is by its failure to budge if you try to remove it. If you aren't sure of the maker's specifications, it's safest to assume that a lag bolt that you can't unscrew is of the anchored type. The only way to remove it is by first removing the heel plate, by applying heat to loosen the glue joint, and then routing out the overlay. Fortunately, there is hardly ever any reason to remove a lag bolt.

Stripped Lag-Bolt Holes

It's also pretty unusual for a lag bolt to strip its hole. If it does, you need to drill out the hole to accommodate a hardwood dowel. Once the dowel is glued in, you can drill it out to a smaller diameter and screw the lag bolt back in.

Dowel-Type Rim-Sticks

Older banjos were constructed with a single wood rim-stick. You'll also see this design on Harmonies and some other modern banjos as well. Usually the dowel was square, and it superficially appeared to be carved out of the same piece of wood as the rest of the neck. Some cheap banjos

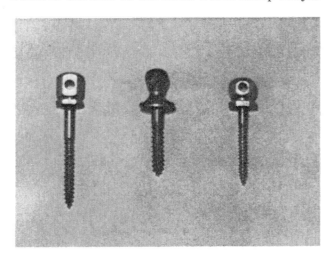

Tailpiece bracket shoes for wooden rim-sticks.

may have used a flat joint, but the rim-stick was mortized in on the better instruments. You may also find one where the rim-stick is keyed in with a dowel. These types of rim-stick are usually held against the lower end of the rim by a bolt with a drilled-through head that also holds the tailpiece bracket.

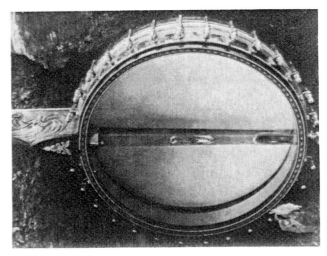

A Whyte Laydie rim-stick.

Sometimes the end of the rim-stick fits flush against the rim, but on some more finely made instruments it sits (without being glued) in a mortise joint. At the upper end of the rim, the stick passes through a hole.

The rim-stick is held tight to the inside of the rim by a screw-tightened *tension bracket* as in the photo above. The photo below shows a more primitive version of this device, where pressure is changed not by turning the screw but by adjusting the tapered hardwood shims between the bracket and the rim. The function of these devices is to provide rigidity in the heel abutment and across the diameter of the rim. You can usually obtain only the most minimal change in neck-angle without making additional changes to adjust the angle of the entire neck/rim-stick structure.

Adjusting Dowel-Type Rim-Stick for Neck Angle

On the finest banjos, such as the Whyte Laydie shown above, the rim-stick hole was of narrow tolerance. Notice also the nickel-silver mortise sheath that protects the integrity of the wood at the lower end of the rim-stick—the rim-stick alone on this beautiful instrument is a work of art.

You can make small changes in the neck-angle of a banjo with an old-fashioned rim-stick simply by shimming between the neck and rim. Too thick a shim, however, puts unbearable pressure on the rim-stick and may also begin to pull the rim out of round. If the banjo requires more of a change in neck-angle than a small shim will provide, you must remove the rim-stick and reglue it at a different angle.

On a banjo that is less finely made, with a less snug hole in the rim and no mortise joint down towards the tailpiece, you have enough leeway to monkey around a little more. The photo at right shows how the neck on one old banjo has been set back by carving out a bit of wood from the end of the rim-stick in order to seat an angle bracket. (It then became necessary to replace the

Angle bracket used to adjust rim-stick angle.

Rim-stick of a Van Eps ragtime banjo. Note the resonator mounting bracket on the middle of the rim-stick.

original tailpiece bracket-shoe, which screwed into the end of the rim-stick, with a bolted-on shoe.) Depending on the size of the angle-bracket and on the desired angle of adjustment, you may be able to simply screw on the bracket without having to carve out any wood. In fact, some banjos are built this way to begin with.

Another variation on this approach is to drill out the screw-hole in the end of the rim-stick and glue in a section of hardwood dowel. You can then drill out a new hole above or below the old one to hold the rim-stick to the desired angle. If the change in angle is so great that the rim-stick isn't wide enough, glue a hardwood block to the rim-stick and drill out the new hole in the block.

Removing and Replacing Dowel-Type Rim-Sticks

If the rim-stick is attached to the neck-heel by a flat joint or in a mortise joint, you should be able to remove it by applying heat and hot water to loosen the glue. If it just won't come, or if it is keyed in with a dowel, then you may be reduced to sawing it off. If this is the case, key it in again with a dowel when you replace it. Drill out holes in both ends of the joint to receive a hardwood dowel large enough to stabilize the joint, and glue it in. An alternative is to rout out a new mortise joint and carve a new rim-stick to fit. However, most rim-sticks bear the maker's imprint and serial number, and should be preserved.

Chapter IX
THE NUT AND BRIDGE: BEARING POINTS OF THE STRING

The Nut

The *nut* is the wood, plastic, bone, or ivory block set at the lower end of the fingerboard just above the peghead, notched with grooves for the strings to rest in. Ivoroid plastic is now the most common nut material, and it is said to have the same acoustic properties as ivory. This is questionable, since it is much softer. Whatever its acoustic properties, it wears down under the strings faster than bone and ivory do. When the strings finally get loose enough in their grooves that the nut has to be replaced, use bone. Ivory is esthetically the most pleasing nut material, but ecologically the most repugnant. Fortunately you are spared the moral choice: elephants are on the endangered species list and it is no longer legal to import ivory into the U.S. Many repair persons lucky enough to have an existing stock conserve it by refusing to use ivory except for the restoration of the finest old instruments.

Fortunately, bone is also quite hard and does the job well acoustically. Preshaped nut-blanks of bone and plastic are available from suppliers in standard dimensions which may have to be shaped down for a given banjo of unusual dimensions, or you can rough-cut the blanks yourself from larger stock and work them down to size with wood rasp and file, finishing up with fine-grit paper for a smooth surface. On old instruments, when the binding and other ornamentation has yellowed, a glaring white new nut can look terribly out of place. You can "age" a new piece of ivory or bone by steeping it in tea or exposing it to tobacco smoke.

Various woods were used as nut material on the less expensive older banjos. They give a rather soft tone on the open strings, which can lead to an annoying discrepancy between a soft open note and a brighter fretted note. If this is happening and it bothers you, replace the wood with bone. A wooden nut is standard on fretless banjos, though, because the "fretted" notes will have the same soft quality.

Removing and Replacing Nuts

The usual way to get a nut off is by applying brute force. Lay a hardwood cushioning block on top of the fingerboard next to the nut and give it a decisive blow with a plastic-tipped mallet. If you have any reason to doubt your aim, protect the exposed part of the fingerboard under and next to the block with a piece of cardboard, etc. Sometimes you can dislodge a fret. Since this is the way you can usually expect a repair person to dislodge a nut, regluing nuts with epoxy or cyanoacrylate glue is not a very smart idea. In fact, the nut doesn't really need to be glued except as a convenience to keep it steady when the strings are changed. Occasionally a maker will just set it in place to be held by nothing more than the pressure of the strings. If this doesn't suit you, use polyvinyl or aliphatic resin glue.

Setting Nut-Height

Finding the right nut-height is important for achieving a comfortable buzz-free action. You have to take the player's action preference, style, and choice of string-gauge into account. The easiest way to determine the height of a new nut is to copy the old one, but of course this only works if the old one was of a satisfactory height to begin with. At any rate, the old nut provides a useful model for gauging the approximate dimensions of the rough-cut blank. A good standard procedure to follow for fine shaping is to capo the strings at the 3rd fret and then cut the nut so that the strings just clear the 1st fret. Remember to leave a little leeway for the notches. The third and (more so) the fourth strings tend to vibrate in a wider arc than the first two strings so they should ride a little higher off the fingerboard. Usually this is accomplished by notching the grroves to different depths for each string, but some folks prefer the appearance of a tapered nut that rises slightly towards the bass end.

If by accident you've cut a nut a bit too low (or if an old nut is too low to begin with), you can shim it up with paper, cardboard, wood or celluloid. A thin shim is okay, but too thick a one might permit the nut to tip forward in its seat under string pressure.

A nut that is too high should be cut down; making the grooves deeper is not a good way of handling this problem.

Notching the Nut

The depths of each groove should not be too deep; just enough to hold the strings in place, about the depth of the string radius. It's most pleasing visually when the string appears to sit right on top of the nut. Even more important, you get the best tone and minimize string breakage this way.

Notch the nut when it is in place. The groove should accommodate the string precisely, with no leeway, so you need a fine tool. A *jeweler's needle file* will work for the fourth and third strings; a *violin maker's saw* is best for the two highest strings. Hold the file or saw on an angle to the nut, so that the tool is parallel to the *peghead*, not to the fingerboard. This keeps the pegward end of the string from bearing abruptly on a sharp edge as it comes off the nut, which makes string breakage less likely at this point. It also assures that the string won't bounce around within the groove.

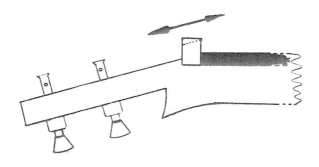

Correct angle for notching the nut: Hold the file or saw along an axis parallel to the peghead.

To space the notches, you can again copy the old nut unless its measurements are not correct to begin with. In that case use calipers, measuring outwards from the center of the nut. Compute a spacing that leaves you with equidistant notches, taking into account that you must leave adequate space above the fourth string and below the first so that the player won't pull the strings off the edge of the fingerboard. Some players need more leeway than others; I can only speak for myself. My own banjo feels fine with the typical dimensions of 3/32-inch leeway on the bass side and 4/32-inch on the treble side. The little bit extra on the treble side helps compensate for the extra movement of the first string as you pull off in a downward direction.

The Bridge

The bearing point of the vibrating section of the string opposite the nut is the bridge. Banjo bridges are moveable, and you have to place them exactly in the right spot in order for the banjo to play in tune (see Chapter III).

Bridges come in two standard heights: 1/2-inch and 5/8-inch. On most brands, the *feet* are thick enough that they can be sanded down for fine adjustment without impairing the bridge's ability to stand up. The typical banjo bridge, and the one most likely to prove satisfactory, is maple with an ebony overlay for the strings to rest on. Some bridges come with two feet, but a three-footed one is best. It will distribute the sound from the middle strings more evenly to the head, and will not sag as easily in the middle.

You can also get bridges with small bone inserts individually set into the ebony under each string. These are supposed to provide a more brilliant tone, but whatever advantage you gain in this respect is more likely than not to be offset by the extra glue joint required to join the bone to the ebony. If you try such a bridge, inspect it for perfectly fitted joints and a minimum of visible glue.

I have also played on an aluminum bridge, which certainly does impart a sharp tone. Apparently there was once a company that made them, years ago. I can't say where to get them nowadays, unless you luck into one on some old banjo. I have also seen but not played on a carved ivory bridge, a lovely old curiosity.

Bridge Height

A maker will put a banjo together with either a 1/2-inch or 5/8-inch bridge in mind, but you can often change from one to the other by altering the angle of the neck. The higher bridge tends to produce greater overall volume because of the increased downwards pressure of the string. (This also depends on the angle at which the tailpiece is adjusted: a screwed-down tension tailpiece can put a great deal of pressure on a lower bridge as well.) Neck-angle and nut-height also affect the optimum choice of the bridge-height, and both of these factors are adjustable as well. Finally, some players just like the feel of one bridge-height more than another for the comfort of their picking hand.

Most bluegrass players like to pick quite close to the bridge; so close that they rest their pinky in the curve of the foot. You can really feel the difference between a high and low bridge when you pick like that, and might quite definitely prefer one to the other.

Frailers have their own peculiar habits. Many like the old-time "rapping" sound where the thumb and index finger strike the head as they play. You can get this sound more easily when the bridge is low and the strings sit closer to the head.

Thinning and Shimming Bridges

Some players—bluegrass, mostly—like to sand their bridges thinner. This makes the tone a little thinner, brightens it considerably, and can also increase sustain. Sometimes you can also use *thinning* to balance out the overall sound, where one string is disproportionately louder or softer than the others: Thin out the wood under the strings that are too loud, and leave it thick under the softer strings. You can also muffle an individual string that sounds too loud or abrasive by putting a little *shim* of paper tape or thin cardboard in the bridge notch (matchbooks get used for this a lot). You'll have to replace it every so often. This is a pretty good trick for curing the kind of overpowering fifth-string sound that you find on many less expensive banjos. You can also work out balance problems by experimenting with different string gauges (see Chapter V).

Chapter X
TAILPIECES

The *tailpiece* is the device that holds the string to the pot. Some tailpieces are fancy with many adjustable parts; others are simple. The simplest I've ever seen is a mere knob that sticks out of the rim. You loop the end of the string around it, pass it over the tension hoop and bridge, and that's that. (It's the bottom banjo in the photo on page 28.) However, most tailpieces fit over the tension hoop, and are attached to a bracket-shoe or rim-stick screw.

Some tailpieces accept only ball-end strings, some only loop-end strings, and others both types. Most of today's banjos come with one or another variation of the classic *Kerschner* or *Waverly* designs as seen in the illustrations below. These are so-called *tension tailpieces* because they have a screw or nut that controls the angle of the tailpiece in relation to the bridge. This determines the amount of pressure with which the strings bear down on the bridge. Another kind of tailpiece is the *finger* or *bear claw* design, where each string has its own mounting, individually adjustable.

Tailpiece Adjustment

A very heavy tailpiece may have a small muting effect on banjo sound, but more important than weight or material for determining the sound of a banjo is the length and angle of the tailpiece. As you crank the tension tailpiece down towards the head and cause the string to bear more strongly on the bridge, volume increases and tone becomes brighter and sharper. For a darker tone (but sharp enough for bluegrass) you can also use a tension tailpiece but adjust it for low tension, angled up away from the head. Listen to the tone of Earl Scruggs and J.D. Crowe; they are both players who don't like their tailpieces (and heads) too tight.

A most unusual instrument: a *mandolin-banjo* from before the turn of the century. Note the banjo-style tailpiece. The instrument, with a five-string banjo neck mated to a flatback mandolin body, bears the imprint of Auguste Pohlmann, but was apparently made by the S.S. Stewart Co.

Low-Tension Tailpieces

The plunkiest-sounding old time banjos come with small, simple tailpieces that are little more than hooks or bars for holding the strings, and they place a minimum amount of string pressure on the bridge. The photo below shows a nicely worked ivory tailpiece that someone once put on an otherwise nondescript mail-order banjo from the 1880s.

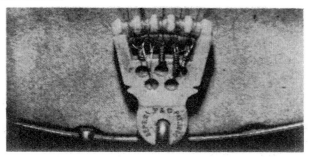

An old, ivory low-tension tailpiece.

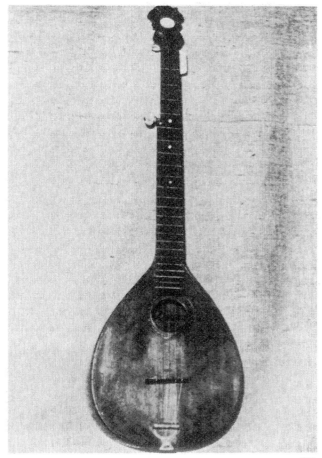

Attaching Strings

Most tension tailpieces, like those pictured below, have a flip-up spring-loaded cover which, when raised, exposes the hooks or holes for attaching the strings. The string must be passed over the main body of the tailpiece and then down underneath through the hole at the end of the tailpiece. In this way the tailpiece can bear down on the string to adjust tension against the bridge.

Three Waverly-style tailpieces, along with a Paramount-style tailpiece (lower right). The tension-adjusting screws are easily visible at the bottom of the tailpieces on the left. The tension of the Paramount-style tailpiece is changed by turning the tapered knob on top.

Sometimes you thread the string through a slot, as in the Kershner tailpiece below.

It's pretty easy to look at a tailpiece and see whether it has hooks (for loop-end strings) or holes or grooves (for ball-end strings). Sometimes you can improvise. Here are some loop-end strings rather gracelessly attached to the protruding feet of a tailpiece that is really intended for ball-end strings.

Low-tension tailpieces on a Van Eps ragtime banjo.

Gold-plated and highly engraved tailpiece on a Vega *Tu-ba-phone Deluxe*. Note the slotted knobs, which accept ball-end strings as well as these loop-end strings—except for the fifth-string knob, which is broken.

Chapter XI
ACTION
AND
STRING BUZZING

The *action* of a stringed instrument is, properly speaking, the distance of the string above the fingerboard; the distance that the string must be depressed in order to produce a note. But people also use the word "action" in a more general sense, to refer to the general feel and sense of playability of the instrument. Used in this looser sense, a number of additional factors besides string-height must also be considered. For example, an instrument strung with heavy strings will feel stiffer to play than an instrument with light strings even if the height of the strings above the fingerboard is the same.

The various factors that determine action, in both the "correct" and looser sense of the word, are all discussed separately throughout this book. The purpose of this one chapter is to discuss them together in one place, to see how they interrelate, and to add some additional perspective.

String-Height

The height of the string above the fingerboard is determined by bridge-height, nut-height, and neck-angle. The *contour* of the neck is also important: string height will be excessive over the middle frets if the neck is warped, and too low over the middle frets if the neck is bowed.

You can feel the effects of *nut-height* most easily when you play on the first few frets, and in open position. Open-string buzzing usually indicates a nut cut too low, or notches cut too deep (which amounts to the same thing). Sometimes, though, the cause will be a fret that has popped up too high in its slot. A feeling of excessive stiffness while playing on the first few frets indicates too high a nut. You can confirm this visually by depressing a string on the 3rd fret. It should just barely clear the 1st fret when you do this; a significant visible gap indicates too high a nut. However, there are some players who prefer the feel of a rather high nut because they play hard, or because they just like the feel of an instrument that asserts itself against their fingers. New banjos usually come from the factory with a rather high nut in order to assure that the instrument will not buzz on an open chord.

Bridge-Height

The height of the bridge increasingly affects the height of the strings as you move further up the fingerboard. Action which is acceptable at the lower frets but too high in the upper positions usually comes from too high a bridge. Action need not be much higher on the upper frets. You could consider a rise of about 3/64-inch between the 1st and 22nd frets to be typical, with some variation depending on the player's preference and the nature of the individual banjo.

Neck-Angle

The angle at which the neck is mounted also affects the consistency of string-height, and sometimes the effects of neck-angle and bridge-height are hard to distinguish. Banjos are like violins and arch-top guitars (and unlike flat-top guitars) in that the neck is set back at an angle so that the nut is actually below the plane of the head. On an instrument with, say a scale of 26¼ inches and a 5/8-inch bridge, the 1st fret might be about 3/8-inch below the plane of the head. If neck-angle changes because the rim-stick slips out of kilter, you may be able to obtain a partial and temporary remedy by changing the bridge-height, but your action will still not feel exactly the way it should until you get the neck reset properly.

Bowing and Warping

Neck distortion leads to inconsistent action in different parts of the fingerboard. Warping (concave distortion) will cause too high an action on the middle frets. Bowing (convex distortion) causes the fingerboard to rise up under the middle frets, so the action will be too low there, or too high over the lower and upper frets. These are the most common forms of neck distortion, but you will also find necks that have a "roller-coaster" contour from alternate bowing and warping, and necks that have been twisted so that the action is lower under the fourth string than under the first, or vice versa. Adjustable truss rods are set to withstand a specific amount of string pressure, and when you go from light to heavy strings, or vice versa, you will often find it necessary to readjust the rod to offset the altered tension.

String-Gauge

Aside from the effect that a change in string-gauge has on the truss rod and ultimately on the neck contour, heavier strings will of course simply *feel* heavier. This may make you want to make small adjustments in nut-height, neck-angle, etc. just to make the instrument feel better to you. Also remember that the thicker diameter of heavier gauge strings will cause them to ride slightly higher in the notches of the bridge and nut, so you may find it necessary to file out the notches a little more.

Tailpiece-Angle

A tailpiece that is adjusted to bear down hard on the strings, moving them closer to the head and increasing the pressure on the bridge, will make the banjo feel stiffer to play.

Scale

If you take two strings of the same gauge and material, stretch them under identical tension, and let them vibrate at different lengths, the longer one will sound lower. The practical effect of this is that the string with the longer vibrating length must be stretched tighter in order to tune it up to the same pitch as an identical shorter string. This means that banjos with a longer scale tend to feel just a bit stiffer.

Fret-Height

A little later we'll consider the effects of a random fret that has popped up too high in its seat, or of an individual fret that someone has incorrectly dressed down without taking into account its effects on the surrounding frets; but it's also possible to find a banjo where all the frets are too low or too high.

There's really no such thing as a too-high fret, but it is possible that a refret job may have been done at some point with frets that have too high or too square a crown for the taste of a given player. The symptoms would be a sense of annoyance in your fingertips, and too much trouble keeping the notes smooth and clear when sliding. The cure is a simple dressing with the fret file.

Too-low frets are easy enough to come by; all you have to do is love to play. You'll wear down and pit your frets, every so often you'll have them milled, and then one day you'll find that you just don't have very much fret left anymore. Too-low frets sometimes make it hard to control buzzing, but most likely they'll just produce unclear, somewhat muted tones. You'll find yourself working awful hard with too-low frets; having to press down with much more strength then you would need with perfect frets. It's easy to see why this is so when you realize exactly how a fret works: The string comes off of the fret against which it is pressed at a slightly upward angle. It has to; otherwise it would vibrate against the next fret. (This is why action rises gradually as you move up the fingerboard.) So, the fretted string looks something like this:

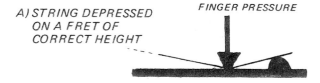

A) STRING DEPRESSED ON A FRET OF CORRECT HEIGHT   FINGER PRESSURE

But if the fret it too low, the finger held in normal playing position won't cause the string to come into sufficient contact with the fret, causing buzzing and indistinct tones.

B) STRING NOT QUITE DEPRESSED ON A TOO-LOW FRET

The insidious thing about worn frets is that isolated tone problems may not be happening often enough, or clearly enough, for you to spot what's really going on. Unconsciously you'll be doing all kinds of things to try to keep your tone good: stretching your finger closer to the fret, rolling around on your fingertip, pressing harder, and so on. Somewhere in the back of your mind you may be thinking that your banjo doesn't sound as good as it used to, or isn't as much fun to play, but it may be many more months before the fretwear really gets bad enough for you to pinpoint the problem.

Trouble-Shooting for String Buzzes

Here is a checklist for the most likely causes of string buzzing, along with a brief description of the possible remedies. Check back to the appropriate section of this book for more complete procedures.

Buzzing on open strings This is usually a symptom of a nut that has been cut or notched too low. It should be shimmed up, or replaced if necessary.

Buzzing on the middle frets This is most likely to be caused by a bow in the neck. Truss-rod adjustment will usually not cure bowing, although this depends on the kind of

truss-rod you have and how it is set, so it's worth experimenting. Otherwise, straightening the neck or dressing the fingerboard is called for.

Buzzing on the lower frets This may be caused by worn-out frets, since these are the frets that get played on most. The frets need to be dressed and, if necessary, replaced. (See also "Buzzing on the lower and/or upper frets" below.)

Buzzing on the lower and/or upper frets This can be caused by a combination of warping and an incorrect repair job. The effect of warping is to make the action too high over the middle frets, where the concave distortion appears. If someone makes a misguided effort to correct this feeling of high action by lowering the bridge and/or nut, or messing with the neck-set, then the action at the lower and/or upper frets will become too low. You first need to cure the warping with truss-rod adjustment, neck straightening, or fingerboard dressing. Then correct the bridge-height, nut-height, and neck-angle.

Buzzing on certain isolated or random frets Sometimes the fret may be simply worn; but often a fret will pop up slightly in its seat. This is often due to expansion and contraction of the fingerboard due to changes in temperature and humidity, though sometimes a maker or repair person just won't have seated the fret properly. Use judgment to determine whether the fret needs to be redriven, dressed, or replaced.

Buzzing on either the bass or treble side of the fingerboard Unless the banjo has been poorly made, it is unlikely that the neck is attached with one side lower than the other. (This is worth checking into, though.) Otherwise, this kind of buzzing is likely a symptom of a neck that has been twisted askew, and needs to be squared. Also check to make sure that the nut and bridge are notched evenly.

Buzzing in several places up and down the neck This could be a sign of an S-curve distortion that is a combination of bowing and warping, in which case the fingerboard must be squared. Very likely the neck was not well reinforced to begin with. If the banjo is a good one, it may be worth the expense or replacing the truss-rod, or of putting one in if there was none to begin with.

Buzzing on all the frets This is an indication that your whole setup is too low. Experiment with different combinations of raising the bridge height and moving up the neck-set. You might also try going to heavier strings. Remember that the harder you play, the higher your action needs to be, even with a perfectly adjusted fingerboard.

Buzzing, rattling, and indistinct tones on the very highest frets Check to see that your strings aren't coming into contact with the tension hoop as you fret them high up the neck. If they are touching the tension hoop or the head, you need a higher bridge and likely a change in neck-set. Another cause of this problem, however, may be a head with too low a crown. This does not allow the tension hoop to pull down low enough to get out of the way of the strings.

Buzzing on one string This may be caused by a neck twisted to one side as described above, but only enough to affect either the first or fourth strings. It may also be caused by an individual bridge-notch that has been cut too deeply under any one of the strings. If there is buzzing on any one open string, check for a nut-notch that is too deep.

An edgy, buzzy quality to your tone in general Try replacing your bridge. Perhaps the notches have become worn.

Hard-to-pin-down buzzes and rattles Some buzzes sound like fret buzzes but aren't really action problems at all. Often it's hard to tell just where the buzz is coming from, and sometimes it sounds exactly as if it's coming from a string even though it isn't. Especially deceptive are the rattles that come from a loose part that vibrates sympathetically only when you play one particular note. Check around for *anything* that could possibly be loose: a bracket, the truss-rod cover, tuners, loose strings-ends, broken winding on the fourth string, etc. Usually the problem isn't serious, but sometimes it can take a couple of weeks to pin it down. Don't neglect, however, the possiblity of a loose or broken truss-rod, which is serious indeed. Tune down your strings and have it repaired immediately.

Chapter XII
THE POT

The word *pot* refers to the entire lower structure of the banjo to which the neck is attached. All the various parts of the pot assembly are discussed separately in the following chapters. This chapter is just to list all the pot parts in one place, so you know what they are.

The rim This is the basic shell of wood or metal to which all the other parts are attached. Cast-metal rims usually include the tone ring in a one-piece casting, but on wood rims the tone ring is separate and detachable. Sometimes the rim is called the *shell*.

The tone ring This is a metal collar that sits on top of the rim and underneath the head. Tone-ring designs range from simple circular rods to complicated semienclosed or completely enclosed air chambers which have a significant effect on tone and volume. Sometimes the tone ring is called the *head bearing*.

The tension hoop This is the metal collar that fits over the outer circumference of the head. The hooked ends of the brackets bear on the tension hoop to tighten the head. Sometimes the tension hoop is called the *stretcher band*.

Bracket shoes or flange Banjos may have one or the other, or a combination of both. They provide a bearing point for the nuts that tighten the brackets.

The tailpiece Some historical banjos have their own unique tailpieces, but as a rule tailpieces are interchangeable and many players prefer to substitute one design for another.

The armrest A metal or wooden flange (or just a simple rod structure) that covers about eight inches of the arc of the tension hoop where the right arm rests in normal playing position. It not only makes playing more comfortable, but also protects the head from wear. Some armrests fit or clip over the brackets, while others are brazed to the brackets. You can easily buy armrests of various sizes and designs from music stores or parts suppliers.

Brazing an armrest permanently to brackets. (Ome. Co.)

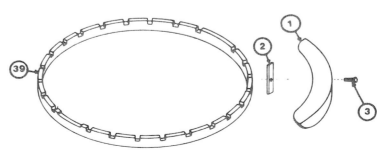

Armrest (1) held to tension hoop (39) with bolt (3) and mounting plate (2). (C. F. Martin Organisation)

Chapter XIII
THE RIM

A good *rim* (sometimes called a *shell*) should be strong and sturdy. Most important, it must be perfectly round in order to accept the tone ring and tension hoop with a good fit. Poor fit of the tone ring results in poor transmission of sound impulses to the rim. Poor fit of the tension hoop keeps it from distributing tension evenly across the head.

Rim Specifications

The standard head size (i.e., outside diameter) of most rims is 10½ inches or 11 inches, with the 11-inch size typical of modern bluegrass banjos. Sometimes you ll run into old banjos with smaller or larger rims; a pretty good number of them were built with rims up to a foot in diameter. They give a bottomy sound which is not very fashionable today. Many of the old rims were not put together in standardized molds, so you find a fairly random selection of rim sizes, in 1/4- and 1/8-inch increments. Sometimes you just can't get a modern standardized plastic head to sit right on one of these old banjos. In that case, you must use a skin head.

The older inexpensive banjos with thin rims, rod-style tone rings, and cheaply cast tension hoops, inevitably distort under rim-stick pressure over the years. Today, after half, going-on-three-quarters of a century, they mostly have egg-shaped rims. Unless you have to replace a broken head, try to avoid taking down such a banjo. They're pretty tricky to get together again.

The size of the inside rim diameter depends upon the thickness of the rim. Many of the old frailers had quite thin rims, down to about 1/4-inch. Most good banjos have a rim thickness of 1/2- to 3/4-inch, and some go to 7/8-inch or more; but this is unusual. For comparison's sake, here are the rim dimensions of a few widely divergent banjo types:

	Rim Thickness	Outside Diameter
Vega Tu-ba-phone # 9 (1925)	1/2"	10 3/4"
Gibson Mastertone	5/8"	11"
Stelling	7/8"	11"
Ibanez Artist	3/4"	11"
Dobson-type (c. 1890)	1/4"	11"
Ome Grubstake	1/2"	11"
Van Eps (ragtime banjo c. 1914)	3/8"	12"

Rim Thickness

The weight and mass of a rim have an important effect on volume and sound quality. Thickness itself is not entirely meaningful, except insofar as thickness means mass. A rim that consists of multiple layers of inferior wood, with many glue joints between the layers, will probably not have better sound qualities than a thinner rim of denser wood and greater integrity. The rim serves as side wall of the air chamber formed by rim, head, and resonator (if there is one). The stiffer the sides of an air chamber, the better its acoustic properties. In addition, the rim absorbs sound impulses, filtering some out and reflecting others back to the head. This affects the nature and duration of the sustained tone.

For the crisp, clear, high-volume sound of bluegrass, you definitely need a thick rim. Few banjos that are good for bluegrass have wood rims less than 5/8-inch thick. (Cast-aluminum rims, which are cheaper and don't sound as good, but which are very good for the price, are thinner.) In part, this is because the thickness of the rim makes for desirable sound and volume qualities. (However, these qualities also come from the total mass of the pot including the flange.) The thickness of the rim is also an important consideration on flange-bearing banjos because the rim, with its machined-out lip, must support the pressure of the flange. (Look ahead at the diagram in Chapter XV to see how different flange and bracket-shoe designs require differently machined rims.)

Old-time playing, on the other hand, demands a completely different response from the banjo. Frailing produces a completely different attack than bluegrass picking does. Even when the old-time player does pick, he will most likely do so without fingerpicks and further from the bridge than the bluegrass player does. And, whereas the bluegrass player rarely strums a chord, brush-strokes are frequent in the old-time frailing and up-picking styles. The result of this is that the crisp brilliance of a good bluegrass banjo often translates into a thin, tinny, and unclear sound under the hands of an old-time banjo player. (By the same token, an excellent old-time banjo may sound slow, lifeless, and cloudy when played bluegrass style.)

Rim design is only one of several factors in the difference between the bluegrass and old-time sound, but it is certainly of great importance. The tone-ring design and the presence or absence of a resonator are also very important (in addition to the various lesser factors considered in Chapter XIX.) The best old-time banjos ever made, the great old Cole, Fairbanks, and Vega banjos, sound fine and loud with rims no thicker than 1/2-inch. Less expensive models went down to 1/4-inch with drilled-through shoe-screw holes, and though they lack the volume and ensemble cutting power of the higher-grade instruments, they really do sound just fine. In fact, many of these older, nondescript and (at the time) inexpensive, thin-rimmed banjos of the period have a more appropriate sound for old-time playing than the finest and most expensive of today's bluegrass banjos.

The net effect is that the frailer can often live happily with a relatively inexpensive instrument, while the bluegrass player must expect to make a more sizeable financial commitment in order to acquire an instrument whose sound is appropriate to his or her style.

Rim Materials and Design

Hardwoods are the best rim woods, with maple and beech preferred. Most rims are visually compatible with the neck in point of wood, staining, and choice of ornamental purfling and binding. On fancier instruments, the bottom edge of the rim may be covered with a decorative binding, which makes the concentric layers of internal lamination invisible. On cheaper instruments, this ornamentation may be left off to save a little cost in labor and materials. On some cheap banjos, the binding will be there to conceal a poorly assembled rim. On many of the thin-rimmed older banjos, the outer edge of the rim is sheathed in a sleeve of spun metal. This

sheath is integral with the tone ring. You'll find further discussion of this design in the chapter on tone rings (Chapter XVI).

Flange-bearing banjos must also have a *lip* around the edge of the rim to support the flange. It may be glued onto the turned rim of a cheap banjo, but on better banjos it is machined out of a thicker rim blank. When you turn out the lip, you get a more precise tolerance than you get by gluing.

By far the most frequent rim design is a *wrap laminate* consisting of from three to a dozen layers of wood steam-molded and glued in concentric circles.

Design of 3-ply laminate rim.

The molds used for shaping rims vary from sophisticated apparatus for mass production down to modified brake-drums used by casual makers. Few people make rims just for themselves, since they are easily available from suppliers. Rim blanks come in different sizes depending on the flange and tone-ring designs for which the rim will be machined.

Laminates are used for rims rather than solid woods because they are actually stronger in this application. They flex a little under rim-stick pressure while still providing rigidity—assuming that the woods are good and assembled cross-grain and with good glue joints. A laminated wood structure will flex a little if it has to, where a solid structure would crack.

Wrap laminates are typical in thick rims, though you will also find various versions of *hex* and *block* laminates as discussed below. The number of plies varies from maker to maker and from model to model. You will often hear it said that thick 3- and 4-ply laminates are not desirable because they distort or disintegrate too easily under pressure. Well, sometimes they do—we're talking about what happens over a number of years. But many classic old Gibson 3-ply rims are still going strong.

On the other hand, 10- and 12-ply rims are certainly undesirable. They are used because the manufacturer saves money on wood if he works up to a desired thickness using many thin layers rather than a few thicker ones. They lack both acoustic and structural integrity, since there are so many joints that you end up with too high a proportion of glue to wood.

Different makers may use different types of glue, but nowadays *resorcinol resin* is probably the most common choice for laminating. Epoxy is also used a lot in rims. Rim jointing is one of the few applications in instrument making where epoxy makes unqualified sense.

On thin-rimmed banjos, you'll sometimes find a single-layer, steam-bent and molded rim as shown in the diagram below.

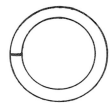

Design of molded single-ply rim.

It's difficult to mold the wood perfectly round. This design is easier to mold.

Design of machined single-ply rim, prior to turning.

The maker circles the bent strip around on itself and glues the protruding end to a mitred corner. Then the protruding end is cut off and the rim machined to a perfect circle.

You'll also find banjo rims constructed out of thicker blocks of laminated wood. The diagrams below show a cross-section of a 7/8-inch Stelling ring, constructed out of thicker hardwood blocks than are found in a rap laminate rim, and a raw hex laminate rim of the type used by the Wildwood company. Six hardwood blocks are set in a clamping jig that applies lateral pressure to each of the six sides. Then the hexagon is machined to round.

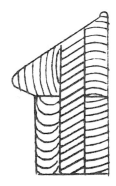

Cross-section of Stelling-type block laminate rim. The blocks are joined by keyed dowels (not shown) as well as by epoxied glue joints.

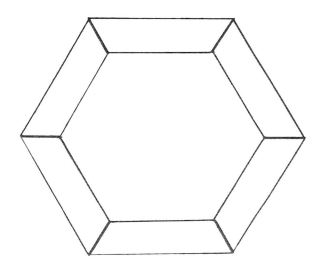

Hex laminate rim-blank prior to turning.

These are the most typical rim designs, but there are more. Mostly the variations are found on cheaper banjos. To save money, a maker might simply glue together random hardwood blocks or sheets into a structure large enough to machine into a rim. This is cheaper than having to buy larger-sized wood sections and molding them prior to machining.

Finally, there is the cast-metal rim. Various metals and designs were used in the past. Nowadays aluminum is generally used, since it is economical, easily workable, and has rather good acoustic properties in this application. Most of today's rim designs are copies or variations of the design developed in the sixties by Chuck Ogsbury, a mountain-dwelling design genius, for his now-defunct *Ode* and *Muse* lines. (The *Ode* name, but not the design, is now used by another company.) This design incorporates a built-in arch-top ring.

The aluminum rim/tone-ring is quite economical and gives a very good return in sound quality for the investment. At the time I write, it's found almost exclusively on inexpensive kit banjos like the Stewart-Macdonald. I don't know why this should be so. Maybe it's because an aluminum rim is nontraditional, not as visually pleasing as wood, and not "organic." Maybe it's just because the very best sounding banjos all have wood rims, and people will therefore be attracted to *any* banjo with a wood rim. Just bear in mind that a good aluminum rim sounds a whole lot better than a bad wood one.

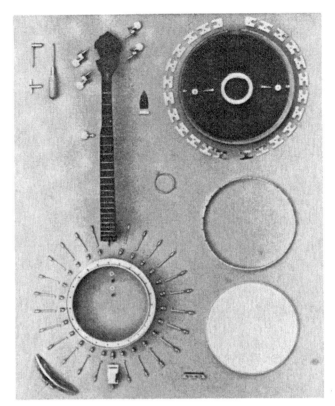

A Saga banjo kit. The cast-aluminum rim/tone-ring is seen below the neck, lower left. (Saga Musical Inst. Co.)

Chapter XIV
THE TENSION HOOP

The *tension hoop* is the circular collar that pulls the head down across the top of the rim and tone ring. It is sometimes called a *stretcher band*. It represents an important historical step in the development of the modern banjo. Very early banjos had no tension hoop. Instead, the head was drawn as tightly as possible across the top of the rim and tacked down. Those old heads must have sounded very flabby by today's standards.

The hooked ends of the brackets fit over the side of the tension hoop to pull it down. As it bears on the head-collar, it tightens the head. The setting of the tension hoop is of major importance in banjo sound, since your banjo will not sound its best unless the pressure is even and uniform.

Tension Hoop Design

There are two main kinds of tension hoop, *grooved* and *notched*.

The difference is mainly cosmetic. Each kind looks and fits best with the appropriate kind of bracket hook, though you can make a substitution in a pinch without sweating it. The hooks for a notched hoop need to be a little squared off at the ends, so that they fit exactly into the notch. A mismatched bracket hook that doesn't fit so well will still do its job; it just won't look as good. The bracket for a grooved hoop, on the other hand, should have a longer and more curved hook so that it grapples over the outside lip of the groove.

Top Tension Banjos

A third kind of tension hoop is the kind found on *top tension* banjos. In this design, there are no bracket hooks. Instead, a bolt mounts with its head in a socket in the tension hoop, and threads in through the flange. That way you can tighten up the head without having to take the resonator off. This must have been quite a boon in the days of skin heads, when people were constantly having to adjust their head tension according to atmospheric conditions.

Grooved (left) and notched tension hoops.

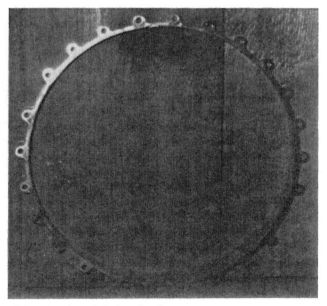

A top tension style tension hoop.

The original top tension banjos were (but are no longer) made by the Gibson company. They were strong and massive instruments. To the extra weight of the tension hoop, with its sockets, was added the attendant weight of the bolts and the heavy one-piece flange that was needed to support them. Added to all this was an unusually heavy, solid (not laminated) resonator—flat inside but carved with a convex curvature outside. The whole banjo weighed in at a hefty fifteen pounds.

Because a large enough number of bluegrass freaks are taken with the top tension idea, a few companies (among them Great Lakes and Stelling) make them on custom order. And top tension conversion kits are available from several suppliers.

Setting the Tension Hoop

Most tension hoops have an indentation which must be set at the point where the fingerboard abuts the pot. The indentation is there so that you won't depress the strings against the tension hoop when you play on the higher frets.

When you set a notched tension hoop, make sure that the notches line up exactly with the bracket shoes or with the bracket holes in the flange. With a grooved tension hoop, you have a little more leeway, since the brackets can hook over the hoop at any point. However, grooved tension hoops tend to become a little scarred at the point where the hooks rest. If your hoop already has these scars, try to line them up with the brackets. That way the bracket hook will fit over the scar that is already made. If the hoop is out of line, the old unsightly scars will be visible, and the hooks will make a new set of scars in a different place.

Tightening the Tension Hoop

A level and uniform tension across the head is one of the most important ingredients in good banjo sound. Fortunately, it's very easy to make sure that you tighten down the tension hoop evenly. All you have to do is work carefully and methodically.

Keep checking the tension hoop visually during the whole tightening procedure. It should never have one side pulled lower than the other. It should always appear level, parallel to the tone ring and the top of the rim.

Start with the first four bracket hooks (as shown below), tightening them only enough so

that they feel secure against the tension hoop, and use only your fingers. There should be no need to use a wrench until the later stages of tightening. If you feel you need a wrench at this point, it means you're tightening too much too soon.

Putting on the bracket hooks in this order makes sure that the tension ring won't get too lopsided. Once the first four are on, add another four in the same fashion.

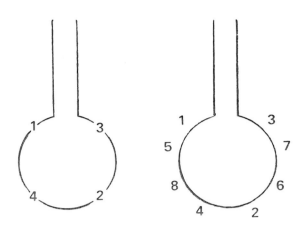

Mount the first four brackets in this order.

Continue to mount the brackets in diametrically opposed pairs.

Keep on going in this fashion until all the brackets are on and bearing down evenly. Then tighten them down again, going back and forth in the same order; first one bracket, then its diametrically opposite partner. Check visually for evenness all the time. Also check the head for loose areas by pushing down with a thumb or finger. If one quadrant feels much looser than another, it requires more bracket tension to bring it even with the rest of the head. (Skin heads sometimes *feel* uneven because their thickness may not be consistent. You can only learn to judge this from experience.)

Use the wrench only when the head is pretty tight. You can probably get the head tight enough with just finger pressure to get it to the point where it will support the bridge without much sagging. Position the bridge and string up the banjo. Then you can listen to it, and use the wrench as you listen to adjust the head tension to the sound you want. As before, continue to work evenly around the rim, tightening the brackets in diametrically opposite pairs.

Chapter XV
BRACKET HOOKS, BRACKET SHOES, AND FLANGES

Pressure is applied to the tension hoop by means of a number of hooked brackets called *hooks* or *brackets*. They are hooked at one end to fit over the tension hoop and threaded at the other. The threaded end fits through either a bracket shoe or a flange, depending on the type of banjo. You tighten up the bracket with a hex nut that bears on the shoe or flange. Some hex nuts come with a threaded hole all the way through them, permitting the threaded end of the bracket to protrude through the nut. Others come with a closed-off end, which is rather more graceful in appearance. Since there is no possibility of the bracket protruding through this kind of nut, one should not use too long a bracket if a replacement bracket is needed. Otherwise, the difference between open- and closed-end hex nuts is strictly cosmetic.

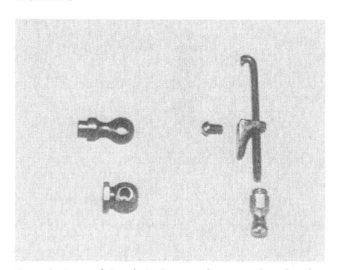

Two designs of bracket shoe, and a complete bracket assembly.

The hex nuts can be turned with any kind of hex wrench of the appropriate size. In a pinch, pliers will do the job, but not without risk of scarring the surface of the nut. The usual kind of wrench is of the skate-key type. Such wrenches are normally supplied with the banjo, or they can be easily purchased from a music store or supply house. Nuts come in a few different sizes depending on the make of banjo, so make sure you get a wrench that matches.

Bracket wrenches.

The brackets must be numerous enough to supply an evenly controlled pressure on the tension hoop. Most banjos have about twenty-four. One bracket for every 1¼-inch to 1½-inch of the circumference is good. Some very inexpensive banjos—old and new—have far fewer brackets. It's one way for the manufacturer to cut corners and you're getting what you pay for. But if price is a consideration, this in itself is not sufficient cause to reject the banjo. In the case of a bracket-shoe style antique banjo, one that has a decent sound but that is not such a classic piece of craftsmanship that alteration is tantamount to desecration, it is easy enough to add new brackets. Simply drill out new holes for bracket shoes evenly between the existing shoes, and mount additional shoes, which, like brackets and hex nuts are easily available from supply houses. Ideally, the new shoes and nuts should match the old ones. If it is not possible to purchase matching shoes and nuts because the old designs are no longer available, then you should consider the cosmetic value of replacing all the shoes and nuts so that they will all be of the same type. Some banjos (a few old Stewarts come to mind) have many more brackets than normal. I'm not sure of the acoustic value of such a set-up. It does lead to a more even distribution of pressure but perhaps unnecessarily so. I think it must have been a sales gimmick rather than a purely acoustic innovation.

There are numerous ways of attaching the brackets indirectly to the rim. The main ones are described below, but from time to time you will see various compromises and combinations.

Bracket shoes These are individual metal receptacles with a hole for the bracket and another hole for a metal screw, called the *rim-screw* or *shoe-holding screw*, which runs through a drilled-out hole in the rim. This is an extremely efficient and at the same time economical way to support the pressure of the bracket hooks. In theory, it has acoustic disadvantages in that the screw-holes interfere with the structural integrity of the rim. Nonetheless, there are many finely made and fine sounding banjos that use this system.

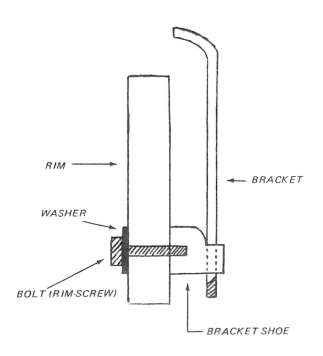

Standard bracket-shoe configuration.

The Vega bracket-shoe system In this configuration, the rim is machined to provide a small overhanging lip beneath which rests a metal collar called the *shoe-bearing band*. The shoes are mounted to this band rather than through the entire thickness of the rim, and so the structural and acoustic integrity of the rim is preserved. In addition, the metal band adds a certain amount of mass to the pot. I have seen an odd banjo or two on which such a metal band is present, but only for decorative reasons, so the mere presence of a metal band around the rim is not by itself a dead give-away that this system is the one being used. The only sure way to tell is by looking inside the rim and noting that there are no apparent screws holding the bracket shoes.

This is the system that was used on the great old banjos (Tu-ba-phones, White Laydies, etc.) made by the Vega company of Boston, but you might see it on some other instruments too. (See photo on page 52.)

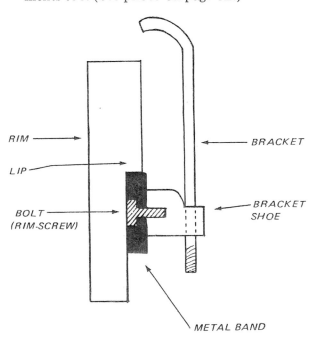

Classic Vega and Fairbanks bracket-shoe configuration.

Bracket and multipiece flange The flange is the circular metal-work piece that fits around the edge of the rim in order to fill the space between the outer circumference of the rim and the inner circumference of the resonator side. As such, its purpose is mainly decorative. In the two subsequent designs we will see how the flange can be adapted to have a structural function also, but this is not the case with the multipiece flange. The multipiece flange is mounted on the bracket shoes, held on by the hex nut. Since it is usually of light mass, and not integral , its acoustic significance is not great.

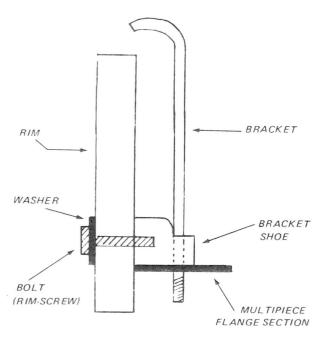

Bracket-shoe and multipiece flange configuration.

Multipiece flange sections mounted individually on bracket shoes on a Great Lakes banjo.

Here is a two-piece flange design:

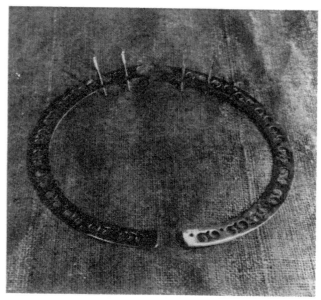

A two-section multipiece flange.

The left and right sides of the flange are mounted onto the shoe brackets just like multipiece flange sections. Here is a similar design with four flange sections.

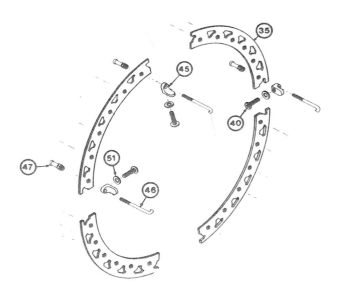

Section of factory blueprint of a modern Vega banjo, with four-section multipiece flange. (C.F. Martin Organisation) (47) bracket nut, (51) rim washer, (46) bracket, (45) bracket shoe, (35) flange section, (40) rim screw.

Given the primary purpose of the flange as a visually pleasing space-filler between rim and resonator edge, flanges are found only on resonator banjos. If you prefer to remove the resonator in order to get an open-backed sound, you'll find that the flange may cut unpleasantly into your thighs when you play in a sitting position. For an easy solution to this problem, use a strap or put a towel or some other cushioning material in your lap when you play. It is more complicated to remove the flange sections. In order to do this, you have to remove the brackets, which loosens the tension hoop and leaves the possibility that your banjo will not sound quite the same once it is back together. This operation is only worth the trouble if you plan never to play with a resonator. In the two subsequent designs you cannot remove the flange, since it serves a structural function.

One-piece flange   In this design, the flange bears against a lip which is machined into the rim; there are no bracket shoes. Instead, the brackets run through holes in the flange and the hex nuts are tightened against the flange itself. This puts a good deal of pressure on the lip, which means that this design can only be used on instruments with a strong and finely turned rim. The flange itself, which may be cast or machined, also bears a great deal of pressure, and it may crack or distort over the years. This was particularly true of earlier flanges made of inferior white metal, and they gave the one-piece flange a bad name. Modern ones, cast in bronze or brass, machined to shape and plated, should hold up better. The heavy weight of the modern one-piece flange is significant enough to affect the acoustical properties of the pot. It tends to make for a more trebly and incisive sound, although, as usual, you can only consider this in the context of the total banjo setup.

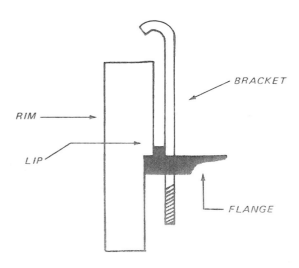

One-piece flange configuration.

Two-piece tube-and-plate flange   In this design, a metal tube bears against the lip which has been machined into the rim, with the decorative flange-plate assembly mounted underneath.

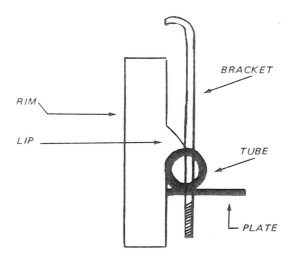

Two-piece flange configuration.

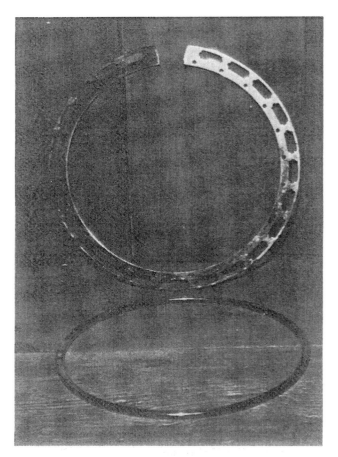

The tube and plate of a two-piece flange.

Thus it is the tube, and not the thinner flange itself, that bears the pressure of the tightened brackets. A tube-and-plate flange runs less danger of cracking or distress than a one-piece flange does. On the other hand, the lip runs a slightly higher danger of cracking. To compensate for this, rims on banjos carrying two-piece flanges are usually made thicker so that a wider lip can be turned. This adds to the expense of manufacturing the banjo, and additional expense is tacked on because the lip of a tube-and-plate-bearing rim must be machined to an extremely precise tolerance.

The tube-and-plate flange will lend different acoustical properties to the banjos, since it is lighter in weight than a good one-piece flange. Sometimes you'll see inexpensive banjos that have two flange plates rather than a tube and plate. This design is cheaper to make and not as strong as a tube-and-plate flange.

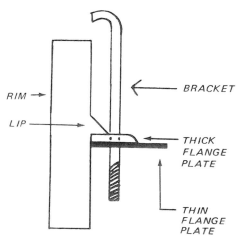

Double-plate flange configuration.

Brackets mounted directly into the rim This is the configuration best known from the cast-plastic rims of Harmony banjos, where the rim design incorporates a lip into which holes for the brackets are set. It is also found occasionally on fine banjos as well. The photo below shows an unusual and superbly made old Weymann rim, thicker at the base than at the top. The bottom of the rim widens out to a lip through which holes are drilled to accommodate the brackets. They are held on by special collared hex nuts which fit into larger countersunk holes at the base.

Heels cut to accept different bracket-bearing configurations. Top to bottom: one-piece flange, shoe-and-bracket, and tube-and-plate flange. (Stewart-Macdonald Co.)

Weymann rim and bracket nut. The protruding nut tightens up into a hole countersunk into the bottom of the rim.

Heel Shapes

On banjos where the flange makes a complete circumference of the rim, the heel is shaped to accommodate it. This means that you can't just casually transfer a neck from one pot to another: you've got to use a neck where the heel fits the flange design of the particular pot you have in mind. If the heel is solid, you must rout out a groove to fit around the flange. If the heel already has a groove that doesn't fit the new flange, glue in a maple plug to restore the heel to flatness, rout out a groove to fit the new flange, and spot-finish around the edges of the plug.

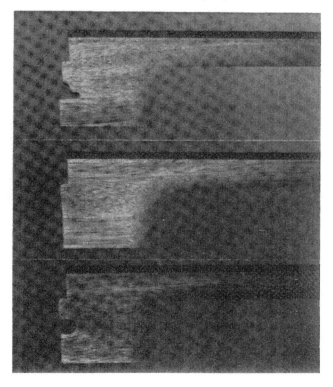

Chapter XVI
THE TONE RING

The *tone ring* is the collarlike bearing that sits on the top edge of the rim. The head is tightened over the tone ring by the tension hoop. There are numerous tone-ring designs which greatly affect a banjo's volume and overall sound. I hesitate, though, to try to pin down a specific sound to any specific tone-ring design: to do so would require language so impressionistic as to be meaningless. Besides, the classic tone-ring designs are all associated with specific types of banjos, which means that you have to take the design and materials of the whole pot into account as well. I'll only go as far as pointing out which designs are associated with frailing banjos and which with bluegrass banjos—and even so, there are plenty of exceptions.

Tone ring designs. Clockwise from top left: (1) cast flat-head tone ring prior to machining, (2) the same design as (1), machined smooth and with drilled-out holes along the inner circumference, (3) a lighter-weight extruded flathead tone ring without holes, (4) a hollow tubular-rod tone ring.

The most important criterion for a tone ring is that is should be perfectly cast of good quality metal, and then machined for a perfect fit to an equally perfectly machined rim. A simple *rod-type* tone ring just sits on top of the rim, or in a fitted groove. But the more complicated designs have a sleeve that fits around the edge of the rim. These rings must fit snugly. A good test is to see whether you can mount the ring by hand. If you have a good hard job of it, the ring fits well. If you have so hard a job of it that you must use a tool to hammer or press, then the ring is too tight; if the job is effortless, the ring is too loose. For just

plain ordinary good sound, a good fit is probably more important than any variation in design.

Brass, a copper and zinc alloy, is the most commonly used tone-ring material. Sometimes tin is added to the alloy, which adds stiffness and resistance to corrosion, and makes for a brighter tone that you might or might not prefer. From time to time manufacturers have promoted *bell metal* tone rings (as well as bell metal tension hoops and flanges). It is difficult to know what they mean by this unless they specifically state the metallurgic composition of the alloy. Sometimes it may be merely an advertising phrase, although it probably means that some tin has been added to the alloy. True bell metal, however, is bronze. Bronze is an alloy of copper and tin without zinc, and it would sound mighty brittle and tinny if it were really used for banjo parts. Your best bet is not to be misled by a fancy term like *bell metal*. Just listen to the sound of the banjo itself—that will tell you all you need to know.

On cheaper banjos, the tone ring (and other metal parts) might be made of steel, aluminum, or white metal. Or on some very cheap instruments, plastic. All these materials (yes, plastic too) can be chrome plated so as to be indistinguishable to the eye from chrome plated brass.

The earliest banjos were constructed without any tone ring at all. The top of the rim was rounded off to keep the head from tearing, or it was turned with a beveled lip, and that was it. The simplest tone-ring design is a collar of round brass rod that rests on top of the rim.

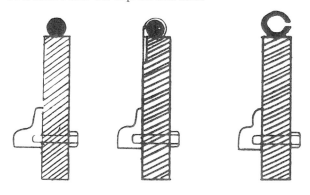

Rod-type tone rings. Left to right: Solid rod, solid rod with spun metal sleeve, and hollow tubular rod with drilled-out hole.

These simple, early rings were often called *head bearings*, indicating that the original concept was not to control sound at all, but merely to provide a smooth, moisture-resistant surface for the head to rest on. This photo shows what is probably the first true tone ring, a Dobson Bros. patent from the 1880s.

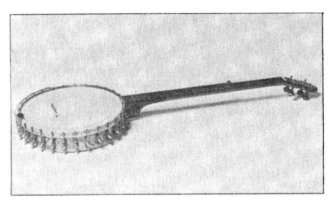

Van Eps arch-top banjo.

The first classic tone ring design: a convex collar bearing a Dobson patent.

The simple, brass-rod collar has remained an efficient, effective, and economical choice of design until the present day. Two variations are also in common use: a hollow brass rod of larger diameter, and the same hollow brass rod, but this time with drilled-out holes along the inner circumference. Rod-type tone rings are most often found on frailing banjos. The next few designs represent further variations.

This photo shows an arch-top banjo that probably dates from the period just before the First World War. It was made by Fred Van Eps, one of the foremost ragtime banjo perfomers of the time and the father of guitarist George Van Eps. This banjo was almost certainly intended for

gut strings, which is to say that it is built to be very responsive to a soft touch, as well as resonant even though the head wasn't driven hard. In addition, as a professional instrument, it had to be rich in the lower register without sounding thin on the high notes.

Van Eps's solution was to use a 12-inch rim; a good inch larger in diameter than a standard rim. This feature alone would increase bass response, but at the expense of clarity. Therefore, he added an arched tone-ring, cast on struts which mounted inside the rim. The arch of the head is clearly visible in the photo above. (You can find photos of the ring design from inside the rim on page 53.) In addition to the arched tone ring, the head also bears on a solid brass rod as it crosses the top of the rim.

The effect of the arch-top configuration is to reduce the diameter of the vibrating portion of the head (which reinforces high frequencies) while at the same time maintaining the large size of the semi-enclosed air chamber formed by the head and rim (which reinforces lows). This is the same principle found in the more elegant, Gibson-style arch-top tone rings discussed a bit later on.

Very often you'll find older banjos with a two-piece tone ring consisting of the solid brass rod overlayed by a brazed-on spun-metal (i.e. lathe-turned) sheath which forms a sleeve around the outer edge of the rim (see diagram on page 79). Many banjos were made with the sleeve running down the whole outer edge of the rim, and brazed around yet another brass rod mounted on the bottom of the rim. Sheet-steel, nickel alloy, and nickel-plated brass were used for this purpose. The sleeve adds mass to the pot and helps distribute sound vibrations through the rim.

This diagram shows a more complicated version of this design, as found on the old Fairbanks *Electric* banjos. ("Electric" was just a model designation- no electricity was involved.)

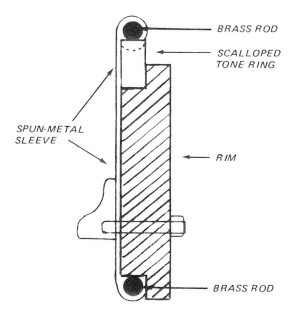

Cross section of Fairbanks *Electric* tone ring and rim.

Fairbanks scalloped tone ring. Other banjos, including the Whyte Laydie, incorporated a similar design.

The same rod-and-sleeve arrangement appears as described above; but, in addition, the upper rod rests on a scalloped metal tone ring. I must say

that these are my favorite old-time banjos, since they combine clarity and balance with a strong, woody tone. However, they sound kind of stodgy; they speak too slowly, add without enough brillance, for bluegrass playing.

You can find another variation of the rod design on the classic Fairbanks and Vega Tu-ba-phones.

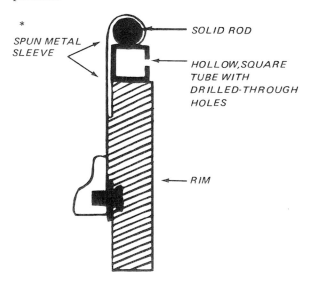

Cross section of Tu-ba-phone tone ring and rim.

Here the rod rests on a hollow, square tube with drilled-out holes along the inner circumference. Like the Electric, these are strong, crisp-sounding old-time banjos.

The classic bluegrass tone ring is the hollow triangle found on Gibson flat-tops and the banjos of many other makers as well. Some form completely enclosed air chambers, while others have

Cross section of flathead tone ring with drilled-out hole, and rim.

* In this diagram, as in all the others in this chapter, the outside of the rim is on the left.

drilled-out holes along the inner circumference. Drilled-out holes reduce the weight and mass of the tone ring, which tends to produce a brighter, crisper sound. (Again, however, comes this warning: Make the final judgment about a particular banjo with your ears, not your eyes.) This tone ring mounts with a sleeve around the outer edge of the rim.

Another classic bluegrass design is the Gibson-style, arch-top tone ring. With one or another slight variation it is used by many manufacturers, and is the kind of tone ring most often found on one-piece, cast aluminum pots. It usually has drilled-out holes along the inside or underside of the inner circumference. As with the Van Eps arch-top described above, this design tends to promote the amplification of higher frequencies because of the smaller diameter of the vibrating surface of the head. There is no end to the debate between flat-top and arch-top partisans. You might as well argue about how you like your food seasoned.

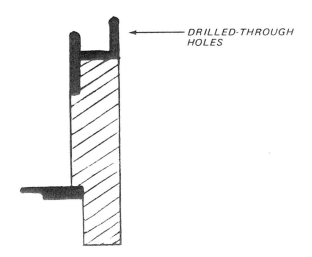

Cross section of arch-top tone ring and rim.

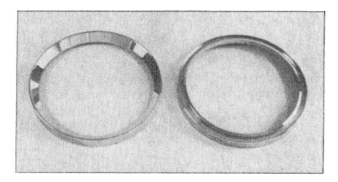

The classic bluegrass tone-ring designs, without drilled-out holes: flathead (left) and arch-top. (Steward-Macdonald Co.)

Ball-Bearing Gibsons

Between 1924 and 1927, Gibson used a *ball-bearing* (also called *floating head*) design on its newly introduced Mastertone line of banjos. This design uses a hollow, tubular tone ring, usually with drilled-out holes. It rests on twenty-four ball bearings mounted on washers (*bearing plates*) and springs which are set into holes drilled into the top of the rim.

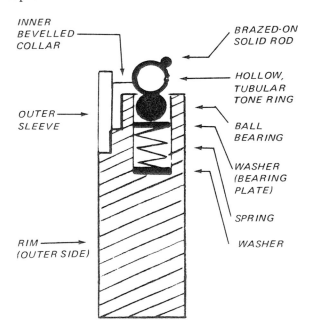

Cross section of Gibson ball-bearing tone ring and rim.

Toward the outside of the rim, the tone-ring tube is supported by a bevelled collar held by a sleeve. Toward the inside of the rim, the tube has brazed to it a smaller brass rod which makes for a sort of mini-arch-top.

The acoustic effect of this configuration is a plunky, hollow sound with a good deal of brightness. A pretty good compromise between a bluegrass and a frailing sound, but with a certain quality that might be described as a bit mushy—at least to the taste of most contemporary bluegrassers. And so, many players like to convert the ball-bearing tone rings to a more typical bluegrass design. My own opinion is that no one should mess with the original designs of old instruments; the limited number of surviving ball-bearing instruments should be reserved for those players who favor them. But this is the conversion procedure:

Remove springs, washers, and bearings. Then drill or ream out the holes slightly to 3/8-inch.

You can then plug the holes with glued-in sections of maple dowel. Then you must sand or turn down the top of the rim 1/8-inch to accommodate a standard Mastertone flat-top tone ring. Alternatively, you can shim up the top of the rim 1/8-inch to accept an arch-top tone ring. You'll also need to glue a maple shim-strip around the outer edge of the top of the rim to fill the space between the rim and the sleeve of the new tone ring. Keep the original parts. You never know—the ball-bearing sound might be the sound of the 1990s.

More Tone-Ring Designs

I've listed some of the main tone-ring designs found on banjos of historical significance. There are more. Some Orpheums used a tube resting on brackets hooked over the top of the rim to create an arch-top effect. Stelling uses a heavy triangle of solid brass. And so on. If you keep looking at banjos, you'll always find one more tone-ring design.

Chapter XVII
THE HEAD

The *head* of the banjo is the flat membrane that stretches across the top of the rim, over the tone ring. The bridge rests on it, and transmits sound impulses from the vibrating strings. These impulses in turn set the head vibrating, which amplifies the sound. In the language of acoustics, the head is a *sounding board*. It is the vibrating surface of the *air chamber* formed by itself, the sides of the rim, and the resonator (if there is one).

Originally, banjo heads were made of calfskin. You can still get skin heads, but nowadays mylar plastic is more common. Other skins can be used too. There are still some old-timers around to tell of their first homemade banjos with goatskin heads. Sometimes people will use the word *skin* to mean any kind of head, be it calfskin or plastic.

Skin Heads

To judge quality in a skin head, look for consistent texture, color, and (most important) thickness. There will always be a few marks or striations, though, since nature always makes patterns. Skin heads are subject to rot, wear, and mildew over the years, so always have an armrest on a banjo with a skin head to protect the head from the sweat of your forearm.

Skin heads are also subject to sometimes alarming changes in tension as they expand and contract from changes in temperature and humidity. Some players are constantly tightening and loosening their heads according to the vagaries of the atmosphere. Others, like myself, just go with the flow unless the head gets so tight that it might split. (Believe it or not, I find that a mushy-sounding banjo on a moist day makes me feel more in touch with my environment.) Early in the century, a few companies tried to market gimmick banjos with low-wattage electric light sockets built into the rim-stick. The idea was that you would plug in your banjo for a while on a humid day in order to dry out the head.

There are still many old-time pickers today who prefer to put up with the moodiness of a skin head. Some are attracted to its characteristic plunky tone. Others use it simply because they are dutiful to tradition. Skin heads are not marketed by gauge—it depends on the calf and, I suppose, on the part of the calf. But if you feel over a few, you'll find that some are thicker than others. Thicker ones sound plunkier, and of course they're stronger too. You'll get a brighter sound from a thinner one, but if bright sound is what you want, you're probably better off going to a plastic head anyway. Most bluegrassers use plastic nowadays, although I read that Sonny Osborne has just gone back to skin. Perhaps he'll start a trend.

Plastic Heads

The plastic heads that have been marketed since the fifties have come to be standard equipment on new factory banjos, and are preferred by most players. They are available in thinner and thicker gauges, depending upon the manufacturer. The thinner gauge tends to give a brighter sound. They also come in several styles.

Clear heads These tend to emphasize brightness and ringiness. Usually they're cloudy and translucent. You can also get them completely transparent, if you like to show off the innards of your banjo. (I personally feel very uncomfortable looking at a banjo with a transparent head.)

Sprayed heads These have a grainy opaque finish, and sound a little more like skin heads. The Remo company has introduced a head with an especially thick grain that is supposed to sound exactly like a skin head, but I haven't heard it yet.

Plastic heads come in several standard diameters. If you have a banjo with an odd-size rim, you might be able to get a plastic head to fit pretty well anyway. Otherwise, you'll just have to use skin. Plastic heads come preshaped with a built-in collar that fits under the tension hoop. The vertical, shaped section between the collar and the flat plane of the head is called the *crown*.

CROWN
COLLAR

Cross section of plastic banjo head.

Heads come in three crown-sizes: high (9/16-inch), medium (1/2-inch), and low (7/16-inch). The crown-height you need depends on your particular banjo. Too high a crown and you may not be able to tighten down the tension hoop enough. Too low a crown, and your tension hoop may ride so high that the strings hit it. If you don't know your crown-size offhand, measure the head when you take it off, or bring it (or the whole banjo) down to the music store when you go to buy a new head. On Gibson Mastertones and on the various Mastertone copies made by other companies, you'll usually find that a flat-head tone ring takes a high or medium crown, and that an arch-top tone ring takes a medium or low crown. Measuring the old head may not be safe, since it may have pulled out of shape: see if there is still a manufacturer's height designation on it.

Since the difference between crown-heights is not great, you sometimes have enough leeway to use one or another. It depends mainly on the rim, tone ring, and tension hoop designs of your particular banjo. It also depends on just how tight or how loose you want to keep your head. Which brings us to:

Head Tension

The more plunk and bottom you want in your sound, the looser you want your head. The brighter and more incisive you want your sound, the tighter you want your head. But it's not all that simple. In order for your banjo to sound its best, your head should be kept taut by an even tension across its entire surface. This is the job of the tension hoop, so take a good look at the section on tightening down the head in Chapter XIV.

Rips and Punctures

Don't panic if you get a small tear in the head. I've kept a plastic head with a 1/4-inch tear in it going for almost two years now by covering it with a small piece of plastic tape on each side. No doubt the banjo sounds a little plunkier and less crisp than it would without the tear, but I'm one of those people who like that sound anyway. I'd certainly replace the head if I were about to take that particular banjo on a performing tour, though. And I don't know how long I'd be able to get away with the tape trick on a skin head.

Replacing the Head

Unless you're a notorious fumbler, you can probably replace a plastic head yourself without any aggravation. But if you can't face up to the task, take it to a repair person. Skin heads are harder: the skin has a will of its own. Don't try to replace a skin head yourself if you can't do calm, slow, and patient work with your hands.

The next four sections will deal with the particular details of getting the skin or plastic head onto the banjo. You'll also need to take a look at Chapter XIV to check on the final steps for tightening down the new head once you get it mounted. For getting either a skin or plastic head off, the steps are the same.

Removing the Head

Start by taking the strings off. This will let the bridge come off too. If you're removing the head in order to put on a new one, then you'll have to use a ruler in order to reposition the bridge correctly (see Chapter III). If you're removing the head for some other reason (like changing to a different tone ring), you'll be putting the same head back on. In that case, you can save yourself the trouble of measuring for bridge placement by marking the location of the bridge with tape or pencil before you loosen the strings. Also mark the head in reference to the fingerboard so you'll replace it in the same place.

If you're planning to change strings at this time, just take them completely off and throw them out. If you want to keep the strings for a while longer, slip a capo over the 7th fret or so: that will hold the strings neatly on the neck. Then loosen them enough to slip them off the tailpiece.

Now loosen the tailpiece. Almost all banjos have tailpieces that are mounted to a bracket shoe (or at any rate to something that looks like a bracket shoe). Just unscrew the nut on the bracket that holds the tailpiece. You need to get the tailpiece out of the way so you can lift up the tension hoop. If the tailpiece swings easily out of the way once it's loosened, just let it swing loose. If it doesn't, then take it off completely.

Now loosen the neck by unscrewing the rim-stick or coordinator-rod nuts (see Chapter VIII). On most banjos, you can replace the head easily enough if the heel is pulled 1/2-inch or so away from the pot, but sometimes you'll find a banjo where the neck has to come off completely in order to give enough space to work.

At this point, you've got the tailpiece hardware off the pot, and perhaps some rim-stick hardware as well. It would be a good idea to start sorting this stuff into some small cardboard boxes so you can keep track of what goes where. Label the boxes if you don't trust your memory. You'll also find the job more pleasant if you cushion your work surface. This keeps the banjo steadier than a smooth surface, and also helps keep parts from rolling around.

The next step is to loosen the tension hoop by unscrewing the bracket nuts (see Chapter XV). Loosen the nuts by stages, first one and then one diametrically opposite it. Work around the rim in this way, unscrewing a little at a time. This makes sure that the tension hoop will come off smoothly, without distorting itself or the tone ring. This is a very cautious way to do this job: if you really know what you're doing, you can use your judgment about whether or not you really have to be so cautious.

Once the bracket nuts are pretty loose, you need to make a decision. If you want to do a quicky job, just slip the hooks off the top of the tone ring and leave them sitting loose in the bracket shoes or flange, with their nuts still on. The other possiblity is to use this opportunity to take down the whole pot, so you can give it a good cleaning. It's a good idea to do this once every few years. In that case, take the bracket hooks off completely. This way you can easily polish up everything—all rim and bracket shoe or flange surfaces, and the bracket hooks and nuts themselves.

Have another box handy to store all this hardware. Keep the nuts with the bracket they came with—screw them back on a turn or two after you've taken them off the pot. You stand less chance of stripping the threads that way, (especially if it's an old banjo, since, in the course of their life, old banjos often pick up a mismatched bracket or two).

Once the brackets are off, just lift off the tension hoop and then the head. If it's a plastic head, you can just throw it away, or try to play frisbee with it. If it's a skin head, save it. You'll need to soak it off its metal collar and use the collar for mounting a new skin.

Mounting the Head

Getting a new plastic head back on is pretty easy. Just do everything you just did in reverse. The new head should fit easily. If you're in doubt about the size, then take the whole banjo down to the shop where you bought the head for advice. Be sure to follow carefully the procedures given in Chapter XIV for tightening down the tension hoop. It's important.

When you mount the head, look for the maker's imprint. If it's on top and looks ugly to you, make sure that you put the head on so that it is hidden by the tailpiece.

Mounting a skin head is more difficult. It's calfskin, but you may wind up believing that it comes from a mule.

Take the old head and soak off the metal collar (also called the *flesh hoop* or *flesh ring*). If the old head was plastic, you'll have to try to buy a flesh hoop. You could also try to bend one yourself out of about 1/8-inch brass or copper rod. Use the tone ring or rim as a mold. A welding shop can set the ends together for you in a jiffy, or you can braze it with a propane torch.

Your new skin should have a diameter approximately 3 inches greater than the rim diameter of your banjo. This gives you some extra material to grab as you fold it over the hoop.

Mounting a skin head to the flesh hoop. (We had to fake this photo with a dry skin. The skin should be soaked and flexible before you do the job for real.)

Soak the new skin in water for a few minutes until it is completely soft and pliable. Then let it lie in a folded towel for a minute or two to to remove excess moisture.

If you've left the bracket hooks hanging loose in their sockets, with the nuts attached, you're in good shape. If you've taken them off for cleaning, then put two or three pairs back in their sockets. Set one bracket of each pair diametrically opposite its partner, and space them out pretty evenly around the circumference of the rim so you can begin to tighten the tension hoop evenly according to the procedure in Chapter XIV. You can do all this while the head is soaking. When you finally get the new skin back on, it will want to slip around a bit, and you'll find the operation easier if you've gotten a head start by having a few brackets already in place.

Now lay the head on a flat surface, with the maker's imprint face down. Place the flesh hoop on top, and center it as well as you can. Fold the margin of the skin back over the hoop, toward the center of the circle, and lay the tension hoop over the fold. Make sure that the tension hoop is bottom-side down. And make sure that the head is tucked in and that you've taken up all the slack in the folds. The flat surface of the head must be completely free of looseness and wrinkles.

Now you're ready to pick up the whole combination of head, flesh ring, and tension hoop, and set it on top of the rim and tone ring. This is a delicate and frustrating procedure, since everything might be kind of slimy by now and the assembly will tend to slide apart. You might have to start the whole procedure all over again. Try to keep calm.

Once you've got the new head over the rim, slip the brackets over the tension hoop and begin to tighten them down according to the method described in Chapter XIV. But don't screw down the tension hoop completely. You need to leave some slack, since the head will tighten itself more as it dries out. Tighten the bracket nuts with fingers only: they shouldn't be so tight that you have to use a wrench at this point. Run a towel around the top and bottom of the head near the rim to wipe up any squeezed-out moisture, and then leave the banjo to dry overnight. After it's dry, you can tighten it down further if need be.

Once the head is completely dry and tight, you'll want to cut off the surplus margin that sticks up over the edge of the rim. Go around the tension hoop carefully with a single-edged *Gem*-type razor or a razor-sharp hobbyist's knife, making certain that you don't cut the sounding face of the head by accident. Then you can tighten up the neck, replace the bridge and tailpiece, string it up, and start picking. Make the final adjustments in head tension with the strings on, so you can hear how it sounds.

Chapter XVIII
THE
RESONATOR

The *resonator* is the platelike gadget that fits over the back of the rim—unless your banjo happens not to have one. In that case, it's an *open-back* banjo. Resonator banjos have flanges, and open-back banjos have bracket shoes.

Some old banjos came with flat resonators that fit pretty tightly over the back of the rim, creating an enclosed air chamber. A few contemporary banjo makers are reviving and experimenting with this design. However, the typical resonator on today's bluegrass banjo has a flat or slightly curved back plus built-in sides that fit around the edges of the flange.

Resonator banjos are standard—essential, as a matter of fact—for the bluegrass sound. At first sight it would seem that the main job of the resonator is to reflect sound vibrations back out through the flange in the direction of the audience. In fact, the resonator does do this, but this isn't really the reason why resonators are so important. The really important function of the resonator is to reflect sound vibrations back against the head. These reflected vibrations hit the head a split second after the original impulse has set the head in motion, so that the note takes on a new sound quality and, most important, sustains longer.

The bluegrass flange-type resonator also makes the banjo louder, especially towards the direction of the audience, whereas the old-fashioned flat resonators mainly affected timbre and sustain. An interesting variation in resonator design was used by the Gibson company on its flat *trapdoor* resonators. The resonator had a hinged section which could be opened or closed to alter the sound. On some instruments the trapdoor was spring-loaded, so that the player could control the degree of aperture by moving the instrument closer or further from his rib cage while playing—sort of an early version of a phase shifter.

You can make a resonator from any material, but the best sounding are made of wood. Most often they're built of laminated wood layers; but some, like those on the old Gibson top-tension models, are massive carved affairs. The surface wood layer is usually the same wood as the neck; or at any rate visually compatible with the neck.

A resonator built of a very hard wood, like maple, tends to produce a brighter sound than one made of softer wood like mahogany. On fine instruments, the large surface area on the back of the resonator can be quite a showpiece for a finely grained section of wood, or marquetry inlaying. Often the edges will be bound in purfling or in celluloid binding material.

Typically, frailers and old-time musicians prefer open-back to resonator banjos. If you have an open-back banjo, you can easily convert it to a resonator banjo unless the rim is of an unusual size: simply purchase a multi-piece flange kit from a supplier and attach the individual flange sections to the brackets between the bracket nut and bracket shoe. Then purchase an appropriate-sized resonator, which you can attach to the flange.

Converting a resonator banjo to an open-back banjo is even easier: just take off the resonator. Unfortunately, you'll be left with the edge of the flange exposed, which looks unattractive and which is pretty uncomfortable if you play sitting. If it's a multi-piece flange, you can easily take off the brackets and remove the flange sections. This means that you'll also be loosening the head in the process. Your banjo may sound a little different once you get done because of the slight loss of pot mass when the flange sections come off. (It might sound a whole lot different if you can't get the head back to exactly the same tension.) If your banjo has a one-piece or tube-and-plate flange, you must leave it on, since it has the structural function providing a bearing surface for the bracket nuts. Multi-piece flanges are merely ornamental. (See Chapter XV.)

Resonator Shape and Positioning

The inside of the resonator back may be flat or curved. A curved back is supposed to focus the reflected sound waves back on the head in a more orderly fashion. Theoretically this may be true, but try to hear the difference yourself.

You can get genuine differences in sound, though, depending upon how far back from the head the resonator is positioned. Some resonators can be repositioned by adjusting the screws that hold them. On others the attaching device is not adjustable for position, so you have to replace the device with another one of a different length, or bend down a bracket, or insert a shim somewhere in the attaching device.

Attaching the Resonator

There are a number of ways to attach the resonator to the rest of the banjo. Most often the resonator attaches to the flange, but this isn't always the case.

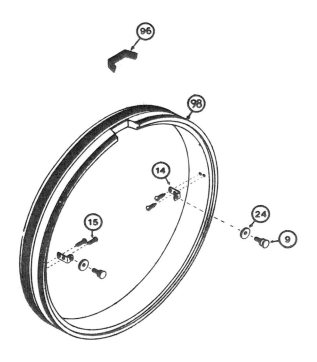

Section of factory blueprint of a modern Vega banjo. (C.F. Martin Organisation)
(15) bracket mounting screws, (14) resonator bracket, (96) cushioning shim for neck, (9) resonator attaching bolt, (24) washer. By adding more washers, or by taking this one away, you alter the distance between the resonator back and the banjo head.

The easiest and sturdiest way of attaching the resonator is by means of four metal screws or bolts that run through holes in the flange into metal brackets that are screwed into the back or sides of the resonator. Instrument makers and suppliers usually call this the *metal-to-metal* system. When you tighten the bolt, it draws the bracket in the resonator tight against the flange. Screw them down with your fingers only: there should be no need to use a wrench or pliers.

On cheaper banjos, you'll see a variation on this design where wood screws run through holes in the flange and into wood blocks glued to the inside of the resonator. The threads in the block tend to strip pretty easily. In that case, you have to dowel in the stripped hole and drill it out again. Or else you can knock and chisel off the old block and glue on a new one. Then you sit and wait for the same thing to happen again. If the flange design permits, you may be able to replace the wood blocks and screws with a metal-to-metal setup. If you own a banjo with this kind of resonator attachment, try not to take the resonator off unless you really have to.

Another way that the resonator may be attached is with springloaded latches that fasten through holes in the flange. It's quick and easy to get the resonator off and on this way, but the fit isn't as secure as with metal-to-metal bolts.

There are also resonators that attach to the back of the banjo. Mostly they are of the flat, non-bluegrass type, but not necessarily so. Some screw into holes in the back of the rim. The old Gibson trapdoors were most often attached in this way. Some have a bolt or screw, set dead center, which attaches to a bracket mounted on the back of the rim-stick (see photo on page 53). If it's a screw, it will usually turn independently of the resonator and will often have a slot large enough to be turned with a dime. (It's comforting to know that a dime is still good for something.) If it's a bolt, you simply spin the whole resonator around to get it on or off.

These are the most common resonator designs. Keep looking, though, and you'll find enough variations and offbeat configurations to fill another chapter. Some of the old Weymann banjos, for example, have spring-loaded pressure clamps, padded with felt, that are mounted around the resonator sides: you get the resonator off simply by giving it a good tug.

Chapter XIX
SOUND AND SETUP

The purpose of this chapter is to provide a brief review in one place of the various features of structure, material, and setup that have been dealt with separately and in greater detail in other parts of the book.

The Banjo Bill of Rights

This is also a good place to gather together the various warnings that appear frequently throughout the book. For while it is undeniably true that the sound of a banjo can be transformed by setup and adjustment, it is equally true that these transformations can be accomplished only within limits. Treat the following injunctions as a bill of rights that will protect not only the integrity of your banjo, but your own sanity as a player and tinkerer as well.

1. *You can't change the basic quality of a banjo.* A cheap or medium grade banjo is less expensive than a fine one because of the cumulative cost-saving effects of every aspect of material, structure, and workmanship. Your time is better spent getting together the money for a better instrument than it is on constant tinkering and parts replacement.

2. *You can't change the basic orientation of a banjo.* The qualities that make, say, a Fairbanks Whyte Laydie a great old-time banjo are pervasive. Adding a resonator and changing the tone ring would ruin the original sound and still leave you with a poor bluegrass banjo. Which brings us to . . .

3. *It is artistically immoral to make permanent decorative or structural alterations on a fine historical instrument.* That's all there is to it—period. *Any* artifact created by an old-time craftsman should be treated as a natural resource. If you don't like the instrument the way it is, you will have little difficulty finding a buyer who does.

4. *A good instrument is no substitute for poor technique.* If you produce poor tone because of a sloppy finger angle, no amount of tinkering will improve your tone. The problem is with you and you're better off spending your time practising, thinking, and observing than you are monkeying with tailpieces and head tension. Of course, you will realize your highest potential on the highest quality, optimally setup banjo, but only if you are prepared to meet the challenge. A fine instrument certainly does challenge you. The clearer the tone *it* can produce, the clearer the tone *you* must produce: the cleaner the sound, the cleaner you must play. Sloppy playing is much more noticeable on a good instrument.

5. *Know who you are.* On the basic level this has to do with the very simple matter of choosing between a bluegrass resonator banjo and an open-back old-time banjo. Most folks pick up the banjo because of a strong initial attraction to one kind of music, so this is usually an easy decision. But there are more complex levels too: If you like traditional bluegrass and hate the modern stuff, you'll want the sound of a relatively plunky flathead, whereas the more piercing sound of an arch-top is associated with the modern sound. If you favor an extremely soft frailing touch you will likely be as happy with a relatively inexpensive, thin-rimmed banjo as you would with the finest old Tu-ba-phone, since light banjos are quite responsive to a light touch but fall apart, sound-wise, when you play too hard. Heavier banjos on the other hand, usually like to be played a bit harder.

6. *Take everything with a grain of salt.* Don't expect miracles from tinkering and parts substitution. If the easiest and most obvious changes leave you with a banjo that is still not satisfactory, start looking around for one that is.

7. *Don't get in over your head.* Don't mess around with a job for which you have no background and experience. Leave it to a professional repair person. Even amateur banjo tinkerers have years of experience, beginning with cheap and broken down instruments. I have also noticed that the typical banjo tinkerer tends to be a person who is involved, professionally or as an amateur, in woodworking, machining, auto repair, or similar, practical skill. Taking down a banjo worth hundreds of dollars is not the safest experiment for determining whether your skills lie in this direction. No repair manual can cover the million and one things that are exceptional, or that are likely to go wrong. And understanding with your mind and understanding with your fingers are two very different things.

Bright vs. Dark
Banjo Sound

For practical purposes, I'm going to divide the spectrum of banjo sound into *bright* versus *dark* sound. A bright sound is one that emphasizes high, trebly tone-qualities, and has a strong cutting edge. The net result is a sound that stands out in ensembles, piercing through the surrounding timbres of guitar, bass, mandolin, and fiddle. It's fairly easy to find a banjo that pays for this quality on the first and second strings by having a relatively weak third string and an even weaker fourth string. Only the finest instruments have a good balance all the way across the fingerboard. The cutting aspect of this tone comes from its thinness. It's sort of like the extreme treble setting of an electric guitar. This can sound quite obnoxious when used by itself in a quiet room, but it can sound quite striking in an ensemble context.

A dark sound is thicker and has a more plunky quality that comes from the absence of a cutting edge. An oscilloscope reading would show smoother curves and a less prominent volume peak on the attack. Banjos with this sound tend to be better balanced from string to string, and to blend in with the ensemble sound. An old-time sound would be at the extreme, while the darker bluegrass sounds come closer to the bright side of the sound spectrum, especially on the attack tone.

The best way to understand a sound is to hear it, rather than read about it. For bright sound, listen to players like Alan Munde and Billy Ray Latham in bluegrass. Some old-time players like this sound too: Wade Ward comes to mind as a player who favored an unusually bright sound for his time, place, and style. The classic exponent of the more bottomy bluegrass sound is, of course, Earl Scruggs. J.D. Crowe also prefers that same quality in his tone. Old-time players who prefer the dark sound are legion. Listen to Tommy Jarrell (on County Records), or Art Rosenbaum (on the Kicking Mule label), if you want to hear some sweet banjo playing.

In deciding between one or another kind of tone you have to take many considerations into account. If you play by yourself most of the time, you will probably find the darker tone more satisfying in any style. If you play in ensembles, you must take the desired ensemble sound into account. Some ensembles—particularly old-time and traditional bluegrass ensembles—strive for a unified texture in which the sound of each individual instrument is subordinated to the sound of the group as a whole. Darker sounds work better here. Another kind of ensemble sound is organized according to the principle of separating the specific sounds of the various instruments. Contemporary electric music most often feels like this, particularly insofar as it is treated in the process of recording and mixing. Modern sound recording of any music tends to produce this layered sound. This, I suspect, is what is responsible for the tendency of contemporary bluegrass groups to favor a texture in which each instrument occupies, so to speak, its own clearly defined space. The bright banjo sound works best in this context.

The following table recapitulates the features of structure, material, and setup that make a banjo tend toward a bright or dark sound. Before you get into it, though, please review article six of the Banjo Bill of Rights.

Other Alterations in
Banjo Sound

Clarity

Some banjos have a sort of hollow, echoey ring to them that makes for a general lack of clarity. You'll hear this a lot on cheaper banjos that sound pretty loud yet don't have good tone. For some reason, this is also the case with many bluegrass banjos—even very good ones—when they are frailed instead of picked. A good way to clear

	BOTTOMY, PLUNKY DARK SOUND	TREBLY, CUTTING BRIGHT SOUND
Rim and Tone Ring	Standard, flathead design for bluegrass; scalloped or Tu-ba-phone designs on thick-rimmed frailing banjos, simple brass rod on thin-rimmed banjos. Larger rim sizes (up to 12-inch diameter) were sometimes used in the past, but are too plunky to most players' tastes. This can be somewhat corrected by incorporating an arch-top tone ring.	As thick and dense as possible. Cast aluminum gives a good, cutting edge, though with less volume, balance, and clarity than a good wood rim. Arch-top tone ring; extra tin content will give an even brighter sound.
Flange	Two-piece on bluegrass banjos; bracket shoes instead of flange on old-time banjos.	Heavy brass, one-piece.
Head	Thicker, frosted head, not too tight. Skin head for authentic old-time sound.	Thin, no frosting, as tight as possible.
Tailpiece	Tension tailpiece should be adjusted for maximum height; i.e., lowest tension and smallest downward pressure on bridge. On thin-rimmed, old-time banjos, use a low-tension tailpiece that rests on the rim or that doesn't extend very far toward the bridge.	Long tension-tailpiece, or one with long, individual "fingers" for each string, adjusted for maximum downward pressure on bridge.
Bridge	Normal, stock bridge (not sanded thinner).	5/8-inch bridge, sanded thinner than normal.
Neck and Resonator	Mahogany neck and resonator for bluegrass; open-back for old-time sound.	Maple, walnut, or other extremely hard woods.
Strings	Heavier gauges.	Lighter gauges.

up the tone is to wad up some material between the head and the rim-stick. I've discovered that a loosely crumpled wad of plastic bags (of the sort you put your vegetables in at the supermarket) does the best job of cleaning up the tone without too much loss of volume. You can move the wad around to find the best sound, with the greatest amount of muting taking place when the wad is right under the bridge. If you want to reduce the volume level more drastically, then use a denser material. Pete Seeger recommends a diaper, for example.

Muting

Sometimes it's pleasing to play the banjo with a violin mute clipped to the top of the bridge. Certainly it is pleasing to your neighbors at 2:00 in the A.M. The different mutes—rubber, metal, ivory, or wood—produce slightly different sounds, something like a dulcimer, or the more celestelike settings on an electronic organ. In a pinch, you can also make an effective mute by clamping a clothespin to the bridge. You can get yet one more sound texture by muting with some material (rubber tubing, for example—or a rolled-up matchbook) under the strings, between the tailpiece and the bridge.

Banjo and violin mutes.

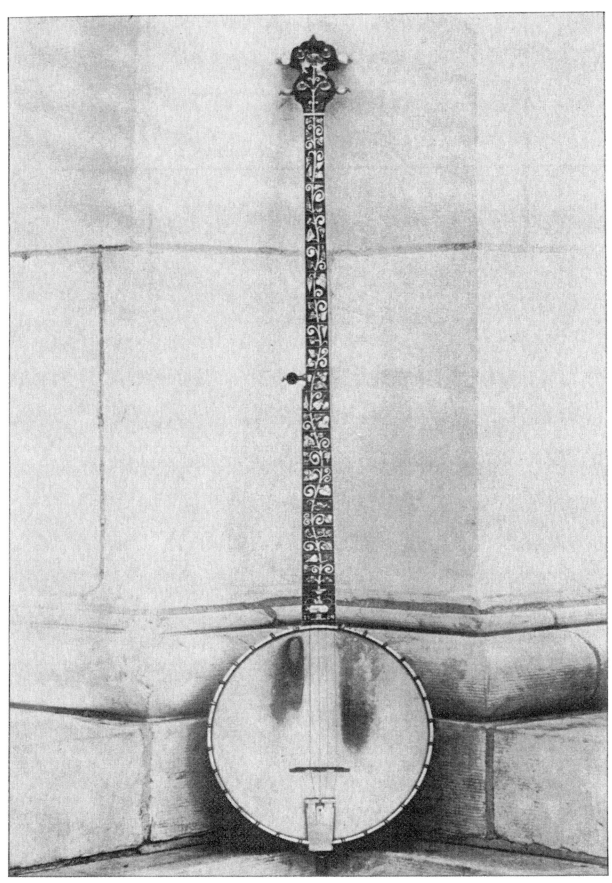

Custom-inlaid banjo with five extra frets, by Ray Chatfield.

Chapter XX
INLAY REPAIR AND REPLACEMENT

Fine and intricate inlaying is a special art. Not every repair person can do it, nor should it be expected of him. By the same token, I have seen a few really bad repair jobs done by craftsmen with justly deserved reputations for fine inlay work. Basic inlay repair and replacement is a necessary skill for all professionals, and intricate work has provided a fine hobby for many amateurs.

Inlay Repair

It will often be necessary to replace inlays that have become loose, or that you yourself have pried loose (with the application of heat) in order to transfer them to a new headstock or fingerboard.

Inlays on fine banjos are customarily cut from *mother-of-pearl*, which is iridescent white, or from *green abalone. Yellow pearl* and other shades of abalone are not traditionally used. I'll be using the word *pearl* loosely throughout this chapter to describe both mother-of-pearl and abalone, as well as the various *pearloid* plastics that are available for inlay on cheaper instruments. These plastics not only lack the visual depth and subtle sheen of true pearl, but are also softer and therefore more susceptible to wear when used on fingerboards.

Pearl is available from suppliers in blocks of various thicknesses. The unit of measurement is called the *ligne*. A 2-ligne thickness, somewhat more than .050-inch, is more than sufficient for most banjo applications and unless exceptional depth of translucency is desired for large inlays, 1½-ligne blocks are more customary. Typical inlay shapes, such as stars, circles, and a few fancy historical shapes, are available precut from suppliers. Otherwise you will have to cut the patterns yourself.

Setting precut inlays. The inlays come attached to the strip of tape in the foreground.

When working for any length of time with pearl and abalone it is absolutely necessary to wear a dust mask over you nose and mouth. At least, tie on a moistened bandana like an old-time outlaw. Pearl contains calcite, which in the short run is toxic enough to leave you feeling unwell, and in the long run can lead to a chronic respiratory condition known as coniosis. Use the mask when working with pearloid plastic too, since it contains pearl dust.

The first step in replacing a missing inlay is to make a template of the original pattern, using the empty hole in the fingerboard, or better yet, copying an identical inlay elsewhere on the fingerboard if there happens to be one. Another way to duplicate inlays is to photograph the neck on a photocopy machine. You will find that the machines at professional copying services work better than the ones in libraries and post offices, and that you will get the clearest reproduction if you bring some heavy cloth to lay over the neck, instead of depending on the rubber flap on the machine. Measure the copy to make sure that the proportion hasn't changed in the copying process.

Tracing an inlay pattern.

but many workers find either the triangle or key-hole shape alone to be sufficient. An *O-gauge* blade is the thickest you should use, going down to 2/0 for detail work. Expect to break blades frequently.

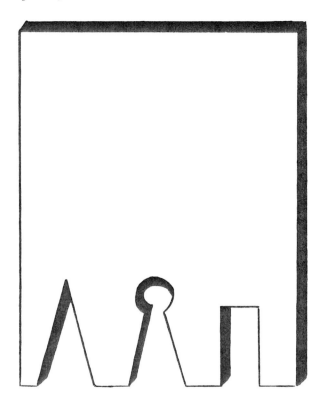

Inlay-cutting jig.

Inlays should be set in a clean smooth hole, so clean the original hold of old glue and any jagged edges of wood and inlay, using a small gouger, dental pick, router burr, etc. If a hole is too deep for the new inlay, make a shim by gluing the inlay block to a thin strip of hardwood veneer before cutting. This is also a good trick for supporting the pearl if you will be cutting it to an intricate pattern that is likely to break. It's likely enough to break even if the pattern is simple, for that matter. If you are just using the shim for cutting support and are planning to remove it, remember to use a low-temperature, water-soluble glue that will come off easily.

Cutting the pattern out of the block comes next. Remember the dust mask. Usually you will be working from a tracing paper pattern glued over the block with an easily removable glue. More rarely you may have occasion to work with a design etched on with a cut-out template, using a needle, small awl, or graver's tool to scribe the outline. Rare is the inlay worker who can trust his draftsmanship well enough to scribe an original outline freehand onto an expensive pearl block.

The cutting is accomplished by using a fine-bladed jeweler's jigsaw working over a *cutting jig* and cutting on the downstroke with the blade pointing downwards. The diagram below shows a cutting jig with three possible cutout designs,

Hold the pearl against the jig with your fingers, since you'll be repositioning it frequently. You might want to use a cushioned clamp for additional support, but don't clamp too tight or you'll break the pearl more easily on the sawstroke. The jig itself should be solidly clamped to the workbench. You must make the sawstrokes absolutely perpendicular to the pearl block and you must be able to work slowly, serenely, and with delicacy in order to avoid shattering the pearl or binding the saw blade on curves. The whole procedure requires a unique combination of firmness and delicacy which some people simply cannot attain. There will be rough edges left over, which can be smoothed with *emery paper* or a fine small file.

Simple inlays that fit exactly into their hole can be easily set with white glue, Duco cement, etc. Complicated patterns will need filler around the hole. (The better an inlay job is, the less filler will be needed.) In this case, set the inlay in epoxy mixed with rosewood or ebony dust. A newly set inlay should be the tiniest bit higher than the fingerboard surface. You can then sand it down flush once the glue sets, along with any excess filler.

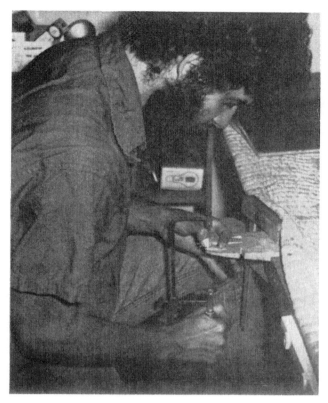

Cutting inlay. Note how rigidly my friend Harry has positioned his knee against the workbench in order to help keep the sawstrokes strong and perpendicular. (If Harry were cutting inlay for more than the few seconds needed to pose for this photo, he'd have to put on a dust mask.)

Original Inlays and New Fingerboards

You can cut original inlay designs as above, once you make up your pattern or have an artist create one for you. Then, the hole for setting the inlay will have to be cut into the fingerboard (or peghead, etc.). In large-scale production, where everything is standardized (especially where pre-cut plastic inlays are involved), a template could be used for outlining the inlay hole. For individual work, though, you'll have to use the cut inlay-piece itself as a template. Glue it with the minimum amount of white glue—at the outer edge of the inlay piece—to avoid any possible squeeze-out, which may mar the finish or the wood surface

around the area to be inlaid. Unavoidable squeeze-out should be cleaned up immediately. To position the inlay exactly, lay out guidelines with masking tape.

Routing inlay holes with a pentagraph machine at the Ome factory. The operator follows the outline of a 200% template on the table in the foreground, which the machine reduces to actual size as the router bit carves out the peghead clamped to the table in the background.

When the glue has set, you will be able to inscribe an outline around the inlay with a needle, graver's tool, etc. Then pry off the inlays with a single-edged razor blade. Work with a piece of cardboard protecting the surrounding wood surface from the blade. Make sure you keep track of which inlays go where when you take them off. Even "identical" pieces will turn out to be slightly different. You may break a piece of inlay as you remove it. If the break is clean, you can simply set the pieces separately, and only a hairline crack will show on close inspection. This is not up to the finest standards of inlay working, but I must say that I've seen it done often enough.

Once the outline is inscribed, you're ready to go to work on the hole with a Dremel tool fitted with a dental burr. Cut just deep enough so that the set inlay will lie slightly above the wood surface, ready for sanding. First use a fine burr to deepen the inscribed outline. That way you'll be able to *feel* the outline as well as see it as you continue to rout out the rest of the hole. Take a break now and then to let the burr cool, or you might see the wood start smoking. Once the hole is cut, you're ready to set the inlay following the procedures described above.

Routing out an inlay hole by hand.

Restoring Engraved Inlay

Many of the fancy old banjos had engraved inlay patterns of dragons, nymphs, etc. The etched lines in the design stand out clearly only when colored by a darker material, which usually wears out by the time it has been played for a half century. To make the engraving visible again, rub in *black wax compound* available from a jeweler's or silversmith's shop.

Two great banjos of bygone times. The inlay engraving is clearly visible on the Whyte Laydie on the left, but the inlays on the Tu-ba-phone on the right need an application of jeweler's wax in order for the engraving to be seen more clearly.

Chapter XXI
TOOLS, GLUES, AND METHODS

You must be properly equipped if you're going to do a lot of banjo work. The right tool for the job is essential for fine craftsmanship.

Make sure you use the right tool for the right job. This saw will probably cut fret-slots that are too wide.

Here's a basic inventory of what you'll need:

Workspace

You'll need a sturdy *workbench* with plenty of surface area. Have a piece of *cushioning material* to cover it—an old blanket, for example. Cushioning protects the instrument and also keeps it from moving around too much as you work on it. A *pegboard* and some small, orderly *shelves* for tools and parts is a great convenience. Strong and adjustable lighting is a must.

Holding Tools

You'll need one or more *bench* and *woodworker's vises*, with wood cushioning-blocks in the jaws. For further protection, you can glue a leather strip over the wood. A small *moveable vise* is also good to have.

A *neck-rest* helps to steady instruments on the bench. (See also chapter XX for an *inlay-cutting jig*.)

A good variety of *pliers*, including a *needlenose jeweler's pliers*, comes in handy. Also a couple of sizes of *Vise-grips*: you'll always find a new application for this handy tool.

Note the cushioned neck-rest right in back of the giant handscrew clamp.

Turning Tools

You'll need *slot-type* and *Phillips screwdrivers*, *nut drivers* in at least 1/4-inch and 3/8-inch socket dimensions, *skatekey wrenches* for bracket nuts, and perhaps *allen wrenches* if you

99

encounter an exotic truss-rod setup. A set of *box wrenches* is also good to have for coordinator rods. You can fake it with pliers, but not without putting some scars on the plating.

Cutting Tools

You'll need a whole arsenal of *snips* and *scissors*, *straight* and *diagonal cutting pliers*, good *wood chisels* and *gouges*, a *putty knife*, etc. A *cold chisel* comes in handy for jobs like getting out a reinforcing rod embedded in epoxy putty. Small, *tapered* (3-edge) *files* and *jeweler's files* are a necessity for cutting notches, trimming new frets, etc. In addition to a repertory of larger *saws* for gross work, you'll also need a *violin maker's saw* and knife, a *jeweler's saw*, a *hobbyist's saw* and a *dovetail saw*. For positioning and regulating the depth of a cut, as in sawing fret slots, some sort of *fence* or *mitre box* is a necessity. You can get one store-bought, or build your own (see Teeter's book in the bibliography). You'll also need a set of *hobbyist's knives*, a *Gem-type single-edge razor* that has a support for finger pressure, a set of *end-nippers* with the outer surface ground flat for pulling frets.

In a large-scale professional shop, power tools like a *table saw*, *band saw* and *jigsaw* become a necessity.

If you do fancy inlay work, you'll also need *scribes* and *fine graver's tools*.

Finally, keep a couple of *kitchen-type table knives* around. They're not much good for cutting, but they have a million uses for prying, as a spatula, etc.

Drilling and Routing Tools

Hand-powered drills and a *hand-held electric drill* are useful for everyone; a professional shop should have a *drill press* as well. A job like drilling out a peghead hole is difficult without one. You'll need a wide selection of *drill bits* too. You can also use the drill press as a buffer and rotary sander.

For routing and fine drilling, the *Dremel Moto-tool* has become a standard item of equipment, and many shops have them in several sizes. They come with a wide selection of *bits* and *burrs*, which you can supplement with burrs from a dental supply shop. Perhaps your dentist has some old ones that are no longer sharp enough for his trade but that will still work for yours.

You can buy a *speed control* for the Dremel tool, or rig your own junction box with a rheostat (i.e. an electric-light-dimmer switch) easily available from a hardware store. You should also get the *removable baseplate attachment* for the Dremel tool. The baseplate helps steady the tool for jobs like cutting out inlay outlines. It's also adjustable as a fence for setting routing depth.

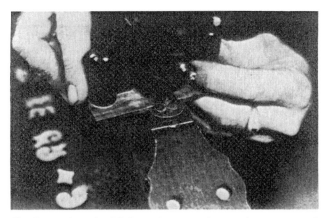

The Dremel tool with baseplate attachment in use to position routing depth. (Ome Co.)

Grinding, Smoothing and Shaping Tools

You'll need a good assortment of *wood rasps* and *wood* and *metal files*. These should include several *safe-edge files* and numerous small files: a *jeweler's file*, *3-cornered slim taper file*, etc. For some jobs a file with a handle feels best. On others, you'll need to hold the file by its main body. Files like this are best mounted on a wood block, with the tang cut off. This is particularly true for the large, smooth *mill file* you'll be using to level frets. If you do a lot of fret work, you'll also find it convenient to cut a 45° groove onto a wood block for mounting a mill file for beveling the ends of frets at the edge of the fingerboard.

Several sizes of *fret files* are available from instrument tool suppliers, too. They most often come with sharp edges, which can damage the fingerboard wood adjacent to the fret. Bevel them smooth on a grinder or with another metal file.

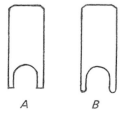

Fret-file cross-sections showing square (left) and bevelled edges.

You'll need a *violin maker's peg shaper* if you do a lot of work with old-style banjos with violin pegs, or if you also work on violins. Otherwise, this is an item of equipment you can put off buying. (Try to borrow one.)

Various grades of *sandpaper* down to 600 grit are useful, along with the finest grade (0000) *steel wool. Sand blocks* help, and for fret work you'll need a large *sanding plane* or *sandpaper file* from an auto body shop. Probably the only plane you'll need is a razor-sharp and finely adjustable *block plane.*

In a professional shop, a *belt sander* and an *electric hand sander* help to get jobs done faster. The electric sander requires an experienced hand, though, since it tends to twist around. It's easy to ruin a fingerboard if you're not used to one.

Measuring Tools

Sooner or later you'll find a use for various *rulers* and *straightedges, calipers* (*vernier* and *divider-type*), *squares, protractors, tape measure,* and even *auto feeler-gauges.*

Heating Tools

A *spirit lamp* is good for neck-straightening, and some repair persons use *infra-red heat lamps* too. A *household iron* is good for loosening frets and joints. Have aluminum foil around to protect the iron from dyes and oils, and some sheet metal for a heat sink. Sometimes frets are easier to get out—especially if they've been epoxied—when you heat them with the point of a *soldering iron.*

Water soluble glue joints come apart easier if you inject hot water, and a *hot plate* is the easiest way to get it. If you have one, you can also inject yourself with coffee when you need it. You can also keep a *double boiler* going for hide glue on the hot plate, though a special *electric gluepot* is worth buying if you use hide glue a lot.

Finally, a *propane torch* is good to have if you want to do your own brazing of metal parts.

Gluing Tools

Spatulas and *brushes* for sure, and *solvents* to keep them clean. You'll also find a *hypodermic syringe* to be a most useful tool for injecting glue into small cracks and hard-to-reach joints; you can also use it to get hot water into glue joints that need to be loosened. Hypodermics are illegal in most places without a doctor's pre-

scription, but somehow most repair persons manage to get a few.

You'll also need a vast array of *clamps: C-clamps, handscrews, spool-type edge clamps, webbing clamps,* etc. (See Hideo Kamimoto's *Complete Guitar Repair* for a good discussion of clamps.) No matter how many clamps you have, you'll always wish you had one more.

Clamps. You'll always need more. (H. Kamimoto)

Storage

Have good storage space and a collection of empty small boxes for holding parts when you're working on a job.

Miscellaneous

You'll need tools to take care of tools: a *sharpening stone* and a *wire file-card.* Have *cleaners, polishes,* and *solvents* on hand, and a *rag-bag* and *paper towels.* Also a box of *scrap-wood parts* for constructing jigs, fences, and supports; and a stock of felt, leather, etc. for cushioning. Finally, *soap* and a minimal *first aid kit* for cuts, burns, and abrasions; and a *dust mask, goggles,* and cloth-and-rubber or plastic *gloves* to help guarantee your safety.

Outside Work

Most shops send out welding, plating, machining and tap-and-die work. Find craftsmen that do dependable, fine work. If you can't trace one down through the instrument repair community, look to antique dealers or a local classic auto club for a recommendation.

New metal parts, to fit standard contemporary specifications, are easily available from parts suppliers. Older parts can sometimes be found by advertising in instrument oriented periodicals (see bibliography). Otherwise, it may be necessary for the accurate restoration of an old instrument to have parts cast at a local foundry.

If you have parts plated, be sure to use the right metal. Keep everything gold if the banjo is gold-plated to begin with. Most banjo parts up to the beginning of World War II were nickel-plated. Since then, chrome plating has been used more often.

Gluing and Clamping

Make all glue joints with care, and protect finished surfaces with masking tape or a cardboard caul. Some glues damage finish, and *any* excess glue bead is unsightly: wipe off squeeze-out immediately. Dried glue can be sanded off or scraped off with a single-edged razor, but never use sandpaper on glue that is still wet. If you ever have to open a joint before the glue has set, clean it up and start all over again. Always leave provision for squeeze-out, since liquid cannot be compressed. In a completely closed joint (such as a keyed-in dowel), leave a little space for squeeze-out in the bottom of the joint.

When you tighten down clamps, use finger strength alone. Using pliers, levers, etc., will result in too tight a set, and you'll squeeze out so much glue that the joint will be weak.

In almost all clamping jobs—especially with metal C-clamps—you'll want to have some sort of cushioning to protect the instrument: leather or felt padding, a wooden caul, etc. For gluing across a large surface area—gluing down a fingerboard, for example—use several clamps applied to a wood platen that covers the entire joint area. This will distribute the clamping pressure evenly across the joint.

Line up all joints and inspect them visually *before* you apply any glue. Clamp up the unglued joint for inspection. Apply glue evenly and completely across both surfaces of the joint.

Glues

Of the numerous specialized glues used in the building and crafts trades, only a few are customarily used in instrument repair:

Aliphatic resin glue is a creamy-colored liquid available in plastic squeeze bottles. *Franklin's Tite-Bond* seems to be the most widely marketed brand. It has almost as good a tack as hide glue, which helps to keep jobs from slipping around too much. It's a fairly good gap filler, doesn't creep much, is water-soluble, and is not affected by lacquer solvents. It has good heat resistance, but not so high that you can't loosen a joint by applying a hot iron, etc. It can be used at temperatures down to 50°F, and at normal room temperature has a shelf-life of about a year. Clamps can be removed after forty-five minutes, but it should set for a day. It darkens light woods slightly. For use with dark woods, it can be darkened with water-soluble dye.

White glue is the casual name for *polyvinyl resin glue*, also available in handy squeeze bottles. The most widely marketed brand is *Elmer's Glue-All.* This versatile glue has become the standard adhesive of the modern furniture industry, and has come to replace hide glue on many factory-made instruments as well. It dries transparent, is water-soluble, may be affected by lacquer solvents, and may begin to creep under conditions of tension, heat, and humidity. Clamps can be removed in ½-hour, but it needs seventy-two hours to set completely. It should not be used in cool temperatures, and, at normal room temperature, its shelf-life is indefinite. White glue has strong shear-strength and impact resistance.

Hide glue is made from cattle hooves, hides and bones and has been the traditional favorite of cabinet makers and instrument builders. With a grip of one ton per square inch, it is almost as strong as epoxy under steady tension: yet it is easy to loosen with heat and hot water. It has poor shear-strength, sometimes enabling one to loosen a joint with a blow or a twist of a spatula.

You can get hide glue from woodworker's suppliers in flake, powder, bead, or strip form. The latter two are less likely to contain impurities. Color ranges from clear amber to dark brown: the darker glue will also dry darker. Follow the supplier's instructions for preparation. This will usually mean overnight soaking in 2 parts cold water to 1 part glue, followed by heating in a double boiler or electric gluepot. The prepared glue should be free of lumps and should drip evenly from a brush. For a slippery job that requires a good tack, increase the proportion of raw glue. For a job that is difficult to penetrate, increase slightly the proportion of water. Apply with a brush, or a moist warm spatula.

Hide glue tacks well and quickly, and takes a day to set. It is water soluble and loosens quickly with the application of heat and hot water. It does not creep under normal conditions, but will give when things get too hot and/or humid. It has excellent qualities as a gap filler, penetrator, and filler of wood pores.

Occasionally hide glue is subject to the growth of a mold that destroys it over a period of years. Ready-made liquid hide glue is available in several brands, with a chemical that prevents mold growth. However, the ready-made glue is inferior in other respects.

Epoxy resin glue is a two-part adhesive. The *resin* and *catalyst* must be mixed in exactly equal proportions on a clear glass or plastic surface. It doesn't creep and, since it hardens by catalytic action rather than by solvent evaporation, it doesn't shrink. Epoxy joints can be unclamped after three hours, but it takes eighteen hours for the glue to cure completely. Some brands may not dry clear, even if so labelled. Epoxy is waterproof, but soluble before it cures with *laquer thinner*. After curing, excess glue must be scraped or chipped off. The separate resin and catalyst tubes have a shelf-life of one year at room temperature. It is an excellent gap filler, and can be darkened with alcohol-soluble *aniline dye*. Dyed epoxy may dry darker than it looks during preparation. Epoxy harms wood finish.

Epoxy is best used for joining metals and plastics to wood and to each other. Other glues are preferable for wood-to-wood joints because epoxy is terribly difficult to loosen once it has set. I view with alarm the increasing tendency of instrument makers and repair persons to go hog-wild with epoxy: apparently it impresses the public. A compromise is to use epoxy only in desperate situations, or when it becomes clear that this is going to be the last time that this particular job will be done on this instrument. For joints that will never have to be undone in the course of a repair job, such as rim laminations, epoxy is acceptable.

Plastic or household cement has the property of melting the plastic edge to which it is applied. In banjo repair, it is used for gluing celluloid bindings and plastic inlays. It creeps easily and should not be used for wood-to-wood joints. *Duco* cement is the most easily accessible brand.

Cyanoacrylate adhesive is the name of the glue you see in supermarkets and hardware stores with a brand name like "Magic Mystery Wonder Superglue" and a picture of one drop holding seven elephants and a Sherman tank to a crane. In fact, it *is* amazingly strong (except under shear pressure) and heat-resistant. It is so strong, and binds so quickly, that its use in most repair applications is limited and tricky. It makes sense for swift jobs that you don't want to clamp, like setting a fifth-string spike or replacing an ebony chip dislodged during refretting. It bonds skin to skin almost instantly, and is a severe eye irritant. Wear gloves, be careful, and keep it where kids can't get it. Cyanoacrylate is acetone soluble.

Resorcinol glue may be used for constructing laminated layers in rims, resonators, etc. It is not usually used in repair applications, though.

Contact cement (*rubber cement*) is sometimes used for attaching sheet plastic to wood, or for bonding veneer to the edge of a laminate. However it creeps easily under pressure and is highly flammable.

Chapter XXII
DAY-TO-DAY CARE

Most of the information in this book has to do with things that have gone wrong. You should also be conscious of the numerous small details that will keep things going right.

Cases

A good many accidents, particularly in the way of impact damage, occur simply because a player has been careless with the storage and transportation of his or her instrument. Any banjo of reasonably good quality should be kept and carried in a good strong case. Fit should be snug, since damage can occur within the case if the banjo has much of a chance to slide around. If your case is too big, you can use a towel, foam rubber, etc. to keep the instrument from moving around. Good cases are expensive, but a worthwhile investment.

Cleaning and Polishing

Keeping your banjo clean is more than a cosmetic task. Most of the gunk that builds up on the surface of an instrument every few months consists of dead skin tissue and sweaty deposits that may ultimately eat away at the wood finish. Besides, a clean-feeling instrument is more fun to play.

There are any number of instrument and furniture polishes that you can use. Some are slightly abrasive, the better to clean off built-up skin and sweat. Others are oily, designed to promote sheen and luster. Keep away from waxy furniture polishes that build up in layers instead of wiping off clean, and from any polish containing *silicone*. Silicone is harmful to glue joints: an accumulation of silicone makes it difficult for new glue joints to take.

Every so often the build-up of dead tissue on the fingerboard will become oppressive. Some people can go for more than a year without leaving much of a deposit on the fingerboard; others need only to play for a few hours. The way to get this stuff off is with 000- or (preferably)

0000-grade steel wool moistened in an oily polish or boiled linseed oil.

Metal parts—flange, tone ring, tension hoop, brackets, and so on—are subject to the build-up of dirt, and consequent corrosion. Do a superficial job of dusting and wiping clean every so often. In the normal course of events you will probably have to dismantle the pot for a head change or some kind of repair or adjustment at least once in a decade; more frequently if you like to tinker. Use these opportunities for a thorough cleaning and polishing of metal parts.

Heat and Cold

Heat is the greatest enemy of wooden instruments. On joints under pressure, hide and resin glues may actually begin to creep at temperatures as low as 110°, although their "official" loosening points are about 50° higher. The trunk or interior of a locked car in the summer sun can easily reach these temperatures, as may a case left in proximity to a radiator, heat duct, etc. Consistent carelessness of this nature can lead to the increasing decrepitude of an instrument over a period of time, even if no dramatic trauma is immediately visible.

Excessive heat and cold can also cause expansion and contraction of various wood and metal structures. Different materials shrink and expand at different rates, leading to cracking, loose joints, loose frets, distortion, and so on. The problem is further exacerbated when the temperature change is sudden. It s a good idea, for example, to carry your instrument in from a cold winter's trip and let it sit in its case for a while so it can warm up gradually.

Air Travel

The airline companies have done a lot to support the instrument repair profession. I am ready to believe at this point that every airline company maintains a middle-level executive whose sole function it is to dream up ways to destroy banjos and guitars.

The best way to travel with an instrument is to get it on board the cabin. Unfortunately, federal regulations do not permit carry-on baggage that will not fit safely under the seat. Exceptions are made solely at the discretion of flight personnel, which means your boarding steward or stewardess. Some companies and personnel will happily try to accommodate you, finding room in a coat-rack or allowing you to strap your instrument into an empty seat. But if there is no room for your instrument, or if the steward(ess) is not willing to cooperate, there is nothing you can do.

Here are some tips for maximum security when flying:

1. Always use a good case. Professionals who travel a lot find it worthwhile to invest in fiberglass or metal-clad cases costing several hundred dollars.

2. Always try to carry-on your instrument. You stand the best chance if you arrive early, before coatroom space is taken up by others. If you have to argue, be firm but courteous. Making an unpleasant scene at the beginning is counterproductive, though you may care to try it as a last resort. Sometimes it works.

3. Insure your instrument beforehand. Many airline companies are now refusing to accept liability at the baggage desk unless the instrument is packed in a case which meets extraordinary criteria.

4. Under no circumstances allow your instrument to be placed on a conveyor belt. This is where the worst damage occurs, and the baggage room is where most theft occurs. If you cannot carry the instrument in the cabin, insist that it be hand-carried to and from the plane's baggage compartment.

5. Tune down your strings before shipping. The effects of many kinds of impact damage are lessened if the strings are not tight.

The relations between airline companies and travelling musicians have just about reached the point of overt hostility since the companies continue to fall back on the assertion that the only way to provide real security is to buy a seat for your instrument. But once war is declared, all's fair. I know one guy who has developed a good subterfuge. Once he gets past security, he puts his banjo case in a hang-up garment bag. (He mounted a dog-leash clamp to the top of his case so he can hang it in the bag.) Then he just walks onto the plane like a travelling executive with a bagful of fancy suits, and hangs the bag in the plane's coat compartment—no questions asked (and none answered).

Insurance and Theft

Insurance is a gamble. I know of one professional with an extensive collection of guitars and banjos who determined what it would cost to insure his instruments and then put the money into a savings account instead. He was lucky. He never had an instrument damaged or stolen, and now after 15 years he has a sizable nest egg.

Others may not prefer this particular risk. For working musicians especially, the loss of an expensive instrument may mean economic disaster. Insurance is available in several forms. The professional, even a part-time professional, should carry a professional policy, which costs more. Insurance companies consistently win court cases in which they can demonstrate that a nonprofessional policy was held by a professional musician, even if the instrument was not lost or damaged under professional conditions. Nonprofessional policies usually consist of a schedule attached to a typical renter's or homeowner's policy. It's hard to find a company which will insure instruments alone except at the professional fee. If you belong to the musician's union, you may find that you can get lower coverage at a group rate through your local.

Insured or not, you should keep a record of your instruments' style designations, serial numbers, and any distinguishing features. The police pawnshop details very often succeed in locating stolen instruments, but they can only do so with adequate information. Photographs can help, too.

On Stage

You wouldn't believe the number of instrument disasters that happen on stage: An amp head falls off a speaker cabinet because the club owner got lazy about nailing in the floorboards securely. Your best friend the mandolin player stumbles back onto the stage after one beer too many during the break. You make a quick switch to guitar between tunes and you set the banjo down right where the dobro player will be rushing between the vocal and instrumental mikes. I never think more acutely about how to protect my instrument than I do in between sets in a club.

Straps

The best, easiest, and most usual way to attach a banjo strap is by tying it with a leather thong, shoelace, or some equally strong material to a couple of the brackets. You'll have to experiment to find just which brackets position the banjo best for you.

Another possibility is to mount a strap button on the underside of the heel, just in the spot where it makes a slightly annoying protrusion against the palm of your left hand if you happen to be playing on the two or three highest frets. (This is where guitar-strap buttons are usually placed too.) Attach the other end of the strap to one of the brackets, as usual. It's easier to get the strap on and off a button, and some banjo players feel that they can position their instrument more stably and more comfortably with one, even though most are happy without one. If you do want a strap button, you can easily find a nickel- or gold-plated one in a music store, complete with mounting screw. Drill out a hole for the screw and soap it up before you mount it, to avoid the risk of splitting the heel. If you have access to a lathe, you can turn yourself an attractive button out of wood, bone, or ivory.

There's one more way to mount a strap—efficient but unsightly. You can mount an eye on top of the heel, and then use a lanyard hook to attach the strap. This provides good balance and easy on/off for the strap, but it looks so ugly that I hesitate to recommend it.

Miscellaneous

There are a few more odds and ends to keep in mind: If you sweat a lot, wipe down the neck, fingerboard, and the pot area around the armrest after every playing session. Keep a clean, soft rag in your case.

If you have a skin head, check it constantly for excessive tightness under hot, dry conditions.

Watch out for belt-buckle damage to the back of your instrument.

Keep your left-hand fingernails good and short—even shorter than needs be merely to play comfortably. That way you'll minimize the wear on your fingerboard over the years. How many times a week do you figure you pull off the third string at the 2nd, 3rd, and 4th frets? Quite a few.

Most important, never forget to treat that seemingly sturdy, and oh-so-heavy, hunk of wood and metal as if it were the most delicate of ancient Chinese vases.

BIBLIOGRAPHY

Periodicals

The following magazines and newsletters often have specialized articles on various aspects of banjo repair, maintenance, history, and reconstruction.

Pickin'. Published monthly by North American Publishing Company. Don Kissel, Editorial Director. Subscription: $12/year (12 issues), $22/two years (24 issues), $30/three years (36 issues). Address: North American Building, 401 North Broad Street, Philadelphia, PA 19108. Phone (215)574-9600.

Bluegrass Unlimited. Published monthly by Bluegrass Unlimited, Inc. Peter V. Kuykendall, Editor and General Manager. Subscription: $8/year (12 issues), $12/year overseas and Canada. Address: Box 111, Broad Run, VA 22014.

Frets. Published monthly by GPI Publications. Roger Siminoff, Editor. Subscription: $18/year, $23/year outside the U.S. and Canada. Address: Box 615, Saratoga, CA 95070.

Mugwumps'. $9/year. Address: 1600 Billman Lane, Silver Spring, MD 20902.

Banjo Newsletter. Published monthly by Banjo Newsletter. Hub Nitchie, Editor/Publisher. Subscription: $8/year, $9/year Canada, $11/year overseas surface, $27/year overseas air post. Address: Box 1830, Annapolis, MD 21404.

Books

Brosnac, Donald
  Tuning Your Guitar. New York: Amsco Music Publishing Company, 1977.

Kamimoto, Hideo
  Complete Guitar Repair. New York: Oak Publications, 1975.

Sandberg, Larry, and Weissman, Dick
  The Folk Music Sourcebook. New York: Alfred A. Knopf/Oak Publications, 1976.

Staff of Guitar Player Magazine
  Guitar Repair Manual. New York: Oak Publications, 1972.

Teeter, Don E.
  The Acoustic Guitar: Adjustment, Care, Maintenance, and Repair. Norman: University of Oklahoma Press, 1975.

SUPPLIERS

Supply-Houses for the Professional and the Serious Amateur

Beacon Banjo Co., 32 Fair Street, Newburyport, MA 01950. (Keith tuners)

Marina Music, 1892 Union Street, San Francisco, CA 94123.

Lewis Luthier Supplies 3607 West Broadway, Vancouver, B.C. V6R 2B8.

Liberty Banjo Co., 2472 Main Street, Bridgeport, CT 06606.

Minalco Products, Box 232, Kensington, MD 20795.

Saga Musical Instruments, 325 Corey Way, Suite 111, South San Francicso, CA 94080. (kits, parts, and accessories)

Rick Shubb, 1701 Woodhaven Way, Oakland, CA 94611. (fifth-string capos and compensated bridges)

Siminoff Banjos. 37 Raynor Road, Morristown, NJ 07960.

Stewart-Macdonald Banjo Co., Box 900, Athens, OH 45701.

H.L. Wild & Co., 510 East 11th Street, New York, NY 10009.

Vitali Import Co., 5944 Atlantic Boulevard, Maywood, CA 90270. (woods, nuts, tuners, etc.)

Music Stores with Mail Order Service for General Musical Merchandise

Andy's Front Hall, R.D. 1 Vorheesville, NY 12186.

Bucks County Folk Music Shop, 40 Sand Road, New Britain, PA 18901.

Denver Folklore Center, 608 East 17th Avenue, Denver, CO 80203. (books strings, records, instruments, accessories)

Elderly Instruments, 541-G East Grand River, East Lansing, MI 48823.

Ferretta Music Service, 82 South Broadway, Denver, CO 80209. (strings, parts, accessories, instruments)

Guitar's Friend, Route 1, Box 541, Sandpoint, ID 83864.

INDEX

Abalone, for inlays, 8
Acoustics, 15-16
Action: and bowing, 61, 62; and bridge height, 61; and buzzing, 62, 63-64; and fret height, 62-63; and nut height, 61; and string gauge, 62; and string height, 61; and tailpiece angle, 62; and warping, 31, 61, 62
Air travel, instrument care during, 105-106
Aliphatic resin glue: described, 102; for fingerboard gluing, 44; for nut, 55; for tuning spike installation, 23
Allen wrench, 34
Aluminum: for bridge, 56; for pot, 82; for rim, 9, 67, 69, 70; for tone ring, 70, 79
Aluminum foil, as buffer, 44
Anchored lag bolts, 51-52, 51i
Angle-bracket, to adjust rimstick angle, 53
Aniline dye, 103
Arch-top tone ring, 80, 80i. 82, 82i
Armrest, 9, 65, 65i
Ash, for neck lamination, 32
Assembly, importance of, 12
Auto feeler-gauges, 101

Backbow, 31. See also Bowing; Warping
Balance: and string gauge, 28; and shimming bridge, 57
Ball-bearing tone ring, 82, 82i, 83
Ball-end strings, 25, 59, 60
Ball peen hammer, 35
Band saw, 100
Banjo Bill of Rights, 91-92
Banjo mutes, 93i
Bear claw design tailpiece, 59
Beech, for rim, 9, 68
Bell metal, 79
Belt buckle, as source of damage, 107
Belt sander, 101
Bench vise, 99
Binding: of fingerboard, 8, 42, 44; flammability of, 42; of rim, 68
Black-wax compound, 98
Block laminate, 68, 69, 69i
Block plane, 42, 45
Bluegrass: bridge height and thickness, 57, 63; flange for, 93; strings for, 28, 93; neck for, 93; plastic head for, 85, 93; players, 92; and resonators, 89, 93; tailpiece for, 93; rim for, 67, 93; tone ring for, 81, 93
Bolt, 74, 74i, 75i
Bone: ageing of, 55; for bridge, 56; for nut, 8, 55
Bowing: and action, 61, 62; and buzzing, 63; causes, 31; definition of, 31
Boxwood, for violin tuners, 21
Bracket hooks, function of, 9. See also Brackets
Bracket nuts, 9. See also Brackets
Brackets: attachment of, 71, 72, 74-75; number needed, 73; removal of, 87; rim-mounted, 77
Bracket shoes, 9, 65, 73, 73i, 74, 74i, 75, 75i
Bracket wrench, 73i

Brass: effect of, on tone, 12; flange, 76; frets, 8; tone ring, 70, 80
Bridge: and buzzing, 64; composition of, 17, 56; compensated saddle for, 17, 17i; function of, 9, 56; height, 9, 56-57, 61, 64; location, and intonation and scale length, 16; marking head for location of, 86; poorly notched, and broken strings, 29; shimming of, 57; and steel strings, 17; thinning, 57
Bright sound, 92, 93 (chart). See also Bluegrass
Broken strings, 29, 53
Bronze, for flange, 76
Brushes, 101
Buzzing: and bowing, 31; sources of, 39, 63-64; and loudness, 39; low frets as sources of, 62; in neck, 32; nut, as source of, 61, 63; on open string, 61; and seasonal changes, 39; and tension hoop, 64

Calipers, 41, 101
Capo, fifth-string, 23, 23i
Capo: for loosening strings, 86; for measuring nut height, 55
Case, for banjo, 105
Cast-metal: pot, 82; rim, 9, 67, 69-70; tone ring, 82
C-clamp, 42, 43i, 44, 101, 102
Celluloid truss rod plate, 33
Clamping: clamps for, 42, 43i, 44, 101, 101i, 102; and neck distortion, 42, 43, 43i; overcompensating in, 43
Cleaning materials, 105
Clear heads, 85
Clothespin, as mute, 93
Cold chisel, 100
Collar, of head, 85, 86, 86i, 87
Complete Guitar Repair, 6, 47, 101
Compound tone, explained, 12
Coniosis, 95
Contact cement, 103
Coordinator rod: changing neck angle with, 51; maximum action adjustment with, 50, 50i, 51i
Cost, of banjo, 12
Crowe, J.D., 59, 92
Crown, of head, 85, 86, 86i
Crowning (rounding), of frets, 40
Cushioning, 42, 99, 102
Cutting jig, for inlays, 96
Cutting pliers, 100
Cyanoacrylate adhesive: attributes of, 103; for filling holes, 21; for fixing fingerboard, 41, 44

Dark sound: 13, 59, 92, 93 (chart). See also Old-style banjo
Diaper, for muting sound, 93
Dimples, of fret, 40
Dividers, for fret placement, 47
Dobson Brothers Company: fretless banjo and fingerboard extender, 48i; tone ring, 80, 80i
Double-boiler, 101
Dovetail saw, 45, 100
Doweling, 52, 53, 83
Dremel tool: for attaching fifth-string

tuner, 22; described, 100, 100i; for fret slots, 44; for inlay work, 97
Dressing, of frets, 40-41, 100
Drills, electric and hand-powered, 100
Drill press, 100
D-tuners, 23-24
Duco cement (household cement): attributes of, 103; for binding, 42; for inlays, 96
Dust mask, 95, 96, 101

Ebony: for bridge, 56; chipping of, 41; for fingerboard, 8, 45, 48; for neck lamination, 32; for peghead overlay, 35; for violin tuners, 21
Ebony dust: for filling chips, 41; for filling inlays, 96
Edge-clamps, 101
Electric gluepot, 101
Electric hand sander, 101
Elmer's Glue-All, 102. See also Polyvinyl resin glue
Emery paper, for inlays, 96
Engraved inlay, 98
End-cutting pliers, 41
End-nipper, 41, 100
Ensemble playing, and sound quality, 92
Epoxy resin glue: attributes of, 103; for filling chips, 41; for filling holes, 21; for inlay filler, 96; for refretting, 44; for rim, 69; for seating frets, 44; solvent for, 103
Equal temperament, explained, 16

Fairbanks: bracket shoe system, 74; tone ring, 81, 81i; Whyte Laydie, 5i, 19i, 52, 52i, 98i
Fence, for cutting fret slots, 45, 100
Fifth string: capos, 23, 23i; composition of, 27; and first-string gauge, 28; shimming on bridge, 57
Files: fret, 40, 100, 100i; jewelers, 56, 100; metal, 100; rasp, 100; safe-edge, 100; tapered, 100; three-cornered slim taper, 100; wood, 55, 100
Filler, for inlays, 96
Finger angle, and tone, 11
Fingerboard: clamping of, 45; cleaning of, 26, 41; described, 8; cutting fret slots in, 45; encasing, for fretless banjo, 48; inlays, 8, 95-98; leveling of, 42; protecting from glue, 44; refretting, 41-42; as reinforcement, 32; relief, 39; removing, 44; removing binding, 41-42, 44; replacement of, 44-46, 44i; squaring, 32, 42, 63; thinning of, 45
Fingerboard extender, 48i
Finger design tailpiece, 59
Fingernails, long, and instrument wear, 107
First aid kit, 101
First string: composition of, 27; and fifth string gauge, 28
Fishing line, for nylon strings, 29
Fixed-pitch instruments, explained, 16
Flange: description of, 9, 65, 74-77; double-plate, 77, 77i; multi-piece, 74-75, 75i; one-piece, 76, 76i, 89; and resonator banjo, 75, 76, 89; and

One-piece flange, 76, 76*i*, 89
Open-back banjo, conversion to and from resonator banjo, 89
Orpheum tone ring, 83
Overtones, 11

Partials, definition of, 11
Parts, locating old, 102
Pearl, thickness of, 95. *See also* Mother-of-pearl
Pearloid plastic, for inlays, 8, 95
Pegboard, 99
Peg dope, 21
Peghead: construction and function of, 7-8, 34*i*, 35, 35*i*, 36, 36*i*; overlay of, 36, 37; and nut angle, 56, 56*i*; reattaching, 36-37, 36*i*
Pegs. *See* Tuning pegs
Peg sharper, 21, 101
Perception of Tone, The, 15
Photocopy, to duplicate inlays, 95
Piccolo banjo, 48*i*
Pitch, defined, 15
Plane: block, 42, 45; sanding, 40, 42
Planetary geared tuners, 20, 20*i*
Plastic: pearloid, 8, 95; for tone ring, 79
Plastic bags, for muting sound, 93
Plastic cement (household cement): attributes of, 103; for binding, 42; for inlays, 96
Plastic heads: dimensions of, 86, 86*i*; gauge and sound of, 85; installing, 87
Pliers, 26, 41, 99
Polyvinyl resin glue (white glue): described, 102; for fingerboard, 44; for inlays, 96, 97; for nut installation, 55; for tuning spike installation, 23
Pot: as air chamber, 12; components of 7, 9, 65; mass of, and sound, 67
Propane torch, 101
Pure tone, explained, 11-12
Putty knife, 100

Rasp, 100
Razor, 88, 100
Reamer, 20, 21
Refretting, 40-41
Reinforcing rod, 8. *See also* Truss rod
Resonator: adding, 89; attaching, 90; function of, 9, 89; parts of, 90*i*; position and effect on sound, 90; woods for, 89
Resonator flange. *See* Flange
Resonator-style banjo, 7*i*. *See also* Bluegrass
Resorcinol resin glue, 69, 103
Reverse bow, 31. *See also* Bowing; Warping
Rim: blanks for, 68; cast-metal, 9, 67, 69-70; described, 9, 65; designs, 68-69, 68*i*, 69*i*; dimensions, 67 (chart), 80; effect on sound, 67, 80, 93; laminated, 68-69; lip, 68; materials used in, 9, 68-70; sheath, 68; single-ply, 69, 69*i*
Rim-screws, 9, 74, 74*i*, 75*i*
Rim-stick: dowel type, 52-53, 52*i*, 53*i*; function of, 49; neck angle and, 49; sheath for, 52, 52*i*; shimming, 53; tension bracket on, 52, 52*i*
Rosenbaum, Art, 92
Rosewood: for fingerboard, 8, 45, 48; for neck, 8; for violin tuners, 21
Rosewood dust: for filling chips, 41; for filling inlay, 96

Rubber cement, 103
Rulers, 101

Safe-edge file, 40
Sand blocks, 101
Sander, power, 45, 101
Sanding plane, 40, 42, 101
Sandpaper, 40, 41, 42, 55, 101
Sandpaper file, 40, 101
Scale: defined, 15; length, 15-16, 46, 62
Scissors, 100
Scrap-wood parts, 101
Screwdrivers, 99
Scribes, 100
Scruggs, Earl, 13, 23, 59, 92
Scruggs-peg, 23-24, 23*i*
Second string, composition of, 27
Seeger, Pete, 46
Serial number, 53
Serrations, 40
Sharpening stone, 101
Shell. *See* Rim
Shimming: of bridge, 57; of inlay, 96; and neck angle, 49; of nut, 63; of rim, 83; of rim-stick, 53
Shoe-bearing band, 74, 74*i*
Shoe-holding screw, 74, 74*i*, 75*i*
Shoe screws. *See* Rim screws
Shubb Capo Company, 17
Single-ply rim, 69, 69*i*
Skin heads: collar of, 87; mounting, 87-88, 87*i*; qualities of, 85; weather's effect on, 85, 107; and top-tension hoop, 71
Sleeve, of tone ring, 80-81, 81*i*
Snips, 100
Soldering iron, 41, 101
Solvents, 101, 103
Spatula, 34, 44, 101
Spirit lamp, 42, 101
Sprayed heads, 85
Spring-loaded latches, to attach resonator, 90
Square fretwire, 40
Squares, 101
Sound: bright vs. dark, 13, 59, 92, 93. *See also* Bluegrass; Old-style banjo; Muting
Steel strings, tuning, 17
Steel wool, 26, 41, 105
Stelling: rim design, 69, 69*i*; tone ring design, 83
Stewart-Macdonald: banjo kit, 70; banjorine, 46*i*; peghead, 34*i*
Straightedge, 101
Straightening jig, 34, 42
Straps, 106-107
Stretcher band. *See* Tension hoop
Strings: ball-end, 25; broken, causes of, 29; buzzing, 31, 32, 61, 62, 63-64; changing, 26-27; cleaning, 25; composition of, 27; conversion of loop-end to ball-end, 59, 60; guitar, 29; heavy, 28, 29, 93; height, factors affecting, 61, 62; loop-end, 25; notches for, 56; nylon, 28-29; old, effect of, 12; removing, 26; replacing, 27; spacing of, 56; steel, and bridge compensation, 17; vibration patterns of, 11, 55-56; winding, 26; wrapping, 26
String-gauge: and action, 62; and sound, 28; *Metric Conversion Table*, 28; *String-Gauge Chart* (Banjo), 27; *String-Gauge Chart* (Guitar), 29

Studs: of fret, 40; for positioning fingerboard, 44, 45

Table knives, 100
Table saw, 45, 100
Tailpiece: and broken strings, 29; finger or bear-claw design, 59; function of, 9, 59; interchangeability of, 65; loosening, 86-87; low-tension, 59, 59*i*, 60*i*; tension of, and action, 57, 59, 62
Tailpiece brackets, 52, 52*i*
Tang, of fret, 40
Tape measure, 101
Tea, for aging bone or ivory, 55
Teeter's method of seating frets, 44
Temperament, 16
Temperatures, effect of, on banjo, 31, 105
Tension bracket, 52, 53, 53*i*
Tension hoop: and buzzing, 64; described, 9, 71; function of, 65, 71; grooved, 71; notched, 71; pressure on, 71; setting and tightening, 72, 72*i*; styles of, 71. *See also* Top-tension hoop
Tension rod. *See* Truss rod
Third string, composition of, 27, 29
Three-cornered file, 40, 41
Thumbrest. *See* Handstop
Timbre, source of, 11
Tobacco, for aging bone or ivory, 55
Tone: color, 11; defined, 15; nut composition and, 55; pure, 11-12. *See also* Bluegrass
Tone ring: arch-top, 80, 80*i*, 82, 82*i*; ball-bearing, 82-83, 82*i*; on cast aluminum rim, 9; early, 79-80, 80*i*; function of, 9, 65, 79-82 passim; hollow triangle, 81, 81*i*; rod design, 79, 79*i*, 81, 81*i*, 82, 82*i*; solid triangle, 83; steel, 79, 80; test of fit, 79; tubular, 82, 82*i*; two-piece, 80, 81, 81*i*
Top tension hoop, 71-72, 71*i*
Trapdoor resonator, 89
Triangle tone-ring, 81, 81*i*
Truss rod: buzzing of, as sign of broken, 64; double-rod design, 33; double-rod removal, 34; fake, 35; function of, 33; installing new, 33*i*, 34-35; Ome Company design, 34; removal of, 34; and string gauge, 62; tightening, 34
Tu-ba-phone: bracket-shoe system, 74; inlay of, 98*i*; tailpiece, 60*i*; tone ring, 81, 81*i*
Tube-and-plate flange, 89
Tuners, *See* Tuning pegs
Tuning, effect of experience on, 15
Tuning pegs: description of, 8, 19-22 passim; fifth-string tuners, 22; friction tuners, 19-20; gear ratios of, 19; geared tuners, 19*i*, 20; guitar tuners, 20; old, 19, 19*i*; parts of, 19; qualities of, 19; violin tuners, 21-22, 21*i*; weight of, 19; worm-and-gear tuners, 20-21
Tuning spike, 22-23
Two-piece flange, 76

Van Eps, Fred, 80
Van Eps, George, 80
Van Eps banjo: arch-top, 80, 80*i*; rim-stick, 53*i*; tailpiece, 60*i*